THE POLITICS OF RELIGION IN AMERICA

Fred Krinsky

Professor
Department of Political Science
University of Southern California

THE GLENCOE PRESS

A Division of The Macmillan Company

Beverly Hills

Preface

Like other volumes in the Insight Series, this book attempts to provide a succinct and cogent exposition of the major problems in one important area of societal development in the United States. In this instance the subject is the complicated relationship between religion and politics. The intent has been not to arrive at specific answers, but rather to pose the pertinent questions and delineate the relevant issues.

The author's introductions provide the context for reprinted selections written by some of the clearest voices available about the questions and historical facts at issue. The first two chapters present the background of church–state relations in the United States with an important excerpt from the writing of Alexis de Tocqueville to balance out accounts by modern historians of religion. The last two chapters concern themselves with contemporary American debates about the separation of church and state and the application of religious moral values in governmental policy. An important part of the presentation is contributed by excerpts from crucial Supreme Court decisions.

The problematic relationship of religion to government may not appear to be particularly pressing at mid-century. Hot- and cold-war policy, racial inequality, and youthful unrest command more space in newspaper headlines, and have almost as long a history among major American problems as church–state relations. But the question of the place and prerogatives of religion in American life, though it is not a crisis issue, is still being posed in many ways.

The author wishes to express his thanks and indebtedness to Michael E. Brown for his help in the preparation of this book.

F. K.

Los Angeles, California
October, 1967

(NOTE.— Throughout this book, the author–editor's footnotes are marked by symbols — *, † — and the original quoted notes by numerals.)

The Insight Series:

Studies in Contemporary Issues

from The Glencoe Press

Problems of American Foreign Policy
Martin B. Hickman

The Oppenheimer Affair:
A Political Play in Three Acts
Joseph Boskin and Fred Krinsky

The Politics of Religion in America
Fred Krinsky

The Welfare State:
Who is My Brother's Keeper?
Fred Krinsky and Joseph Boskin

Opposition Politics:
The Anti-New Deal Tradition
Joseph Boskin

Is American Democracy Exportable?
Edward G. McGrath

Protest from the Right
Robert A. Rosenstone

Democracy and Complexity:
Who Governs the Governors?
Fred Krinsky

Ferment in Labor
Jerome Wolf

Series Editors: Fred Krinsky and Joseph Boskin

Contents

Chapter One

The Wider Context of Church and State

The place of religion within the political state has been a point of conjecture and cause for conflict since the advent of organized and institutionalized religion. There has rarely been a period in the history of the Western world that was not wracked with conflict between religious interests and secular authority.

There are essentially two aspects to the perennial conflicts: (1) *religious ideology* as a competitor with state or empire for its citizens' loyalties, and (2) *institutional religion* as a competitor with secular authority for supreme power in the political process. Christianity in its first several centuries of existence appeared to undermine its adherents' loyalties to existing state authority, what we have of late called "a clear and present danger" to the constituted authority. It was recognized early that ideas can provide germinal motivation and justification for civil disobedience and rebellion.

If it was the threat of an idea that menaced the political system in early Christian history, it was the propagation of the idea and the militancy it engendered that posed the more palpable threat to the state. The rise of the Roman Catholic Church brought with it a well-organized power structure with a growing corps of militants that could be used to intimidate the state. What began as a threat of divided citizen loyalty became, in the Middle Ages, a real power confrontation between the universal Church and the embattled feudal states. Medieval political philosophers were preoccupied with the question of *sovereignty:* who legitimately exercises supreme political power. St. Augustine favored the earthly reign of God's lieutenants through the "two swords" doctrine, the division and sharing of sovereignty. The later Thomistic solution granted to the temporal state dominance over things earthly, and to the Church, the instrument of Eternal Grace, power over things eternal. It was possible for St. Thomas to relegate the Church to moral rather than political power because he envisioned both realms as emanating harmoniously from divine power. Natural law prescribed Justice and Truth as universal qualities, encompassing and delimiting human behavior in every sphere of activity.

Still the basis of Catholic theology, Thomistic tenets have served to ameliorate the conflict over the seat of sovereignty within the state — but by no means have they charted the exact limits of Church power in relation to state power. The Roman Catholic Church, while not directly exercising political power, has continued as a sizable influence on public policy and law in most predominantly Catholic countries. For example, the Church has never really been separated from the state in Italy, retaining its power throughout monarchy, fascist fatherland, and republic. Catholic influence is even greater in other Mediterranean countries and in Latin America.

Inroads on Catholic hegemony came as a result of the Protestant Reformation which swept northern Europe in the sixteenth century. Finally, the Church was denuded of official power in the wake of the eighteenth- and nineteenth-century democratic revolutions. Revolutionary democracy vested sovereignty in the people rather than in hereditary monarchs or religious authority. It conceived of the state as a totally secular affair, ruling to the tune of popular sentiment rather than Divine Law. Ideology aside, revolutionary antagonism to the Church was based upon its intimate accommodation within the *ancien régime*. The overturning of old rulers required that groups that had cooperated with the deposed monarchies should be deprived of political power in the new republics. Each of the new democracies coped in its own way with the religious question, some settling for complete separation, some establishing a state-dominated church, and others attempting pragmatically to accommodate religious forces without resorting to set doctrine.

Protestantism found fertile ground in northern Europe among the rising mercantile nation-states, its individualistic ideology giving rise to a sectarian diversity which prevented Protestantism from welding a unified hierarchical institution capable of recruiting a large enough following to threaten prevailing political institutions. Protestantism was a divided, non-monolithic entity which, by not pretending to universality, was no real threat to the independent, rising nations, except in isolated instances. The Protestant theocracies briefly established in Calvinist Geneva, Cromwell's England, and early Massachusetts, proved non-viable. In fact, the Protestant ethic of hard work, frugality, efficiency, and deferral of earthly pleasures was a positive asset to commercial-industrial development and national prestige. In those nations that adopted a single Protestant denomination as a state religion (e.g. Lutheranism in Sweden), religion in time became totally subordinate to and dependent upon the state.

In the United States of America, the relationship of religion to political state was not a primary question during the constitutionalizing of 1787-89. Colonial Puritan power had waned considerably by the time the states were joined in one union, and a multitude of religious sects were co-existing peaceably with little inclination toward the exercise of political power. The provisions of the First Amendment, guaranteeing freedom of worship and denying state interference by any establishment of religion, were safeguards for the future rather than a statement of intention to change any existing practices. The concern was not that religion might become entrenched as political power, but rather that no future government deny religion the freedom to proselytize freely and to promote the tenets of universal morality.

Thus, while the church–state problem is not the central issue it once was, religion still is a friction point in modern democracies. We might state some of the questions as follows:

1. To what extent are law and public policy based in a "universal" morality and ethics, and to what extent *should* they be?
2. If morality has a place in politics, to what degree should this morality be based in religious values?
3. At what point does the application of religious values to government policy become state support of religion?
4. Does religion have a legitimate right to try to influence politics, and if so, what methods and goals are proper to this role?

These are the questions which, from our contemporary point of view, lie beneath the long history of dispute over church–state relations. As the focus of this book moves more and more directly toward the discussion of religion and politics in the modern United States, such questions will grow more and more explicit and central. But first it will be valuable to take a general look at the pattern of church–state relations in other Western, democratic nations.

Religion and Politics in Modern Democracies*

Leo Pfeffer

Great Britain

Great Britain is frequently pointed to as a country which maintains complete religious freedom alongside an establishment of religion. It is of course true that there is a large measure of religious

---

* From Leo Pfeffer, *Church, State and Freedom* (Boston: Beacon Press, 1967), pp. 52–61, 70. Reprinted by permission of the Beacon Press, © 1953 by the Beacon Press, © 1967 by Leo Pfeffer.

liberty in England; whether there is complete religious liberty depends largely on one's viewpoint. Many, for example, would say that a child in the English common school who must make a specific request to be excused from participating in instruction in which he is taught at home and in church to disbelieve is not enjoying complete religious liberty. So, too, Jefferson, who drafted the Virginia Statute of Religious Freedom, to assure that "no man shall be compelled to . . . support any religious worship, place, or ministry whatsoever," would hardly agree that the English taxpayer who is required to support the Anglican establishment enjoys complete religious freedom. Within our own generation, certain dissenting ministers have gone to jail one day each year for refusing to pay local taxes from which were drawn subsidies for Church of England schools.

Certainly the established church does not enjoy religious freedom — at least that is the testimony of the two English archbishops. In the preface to his *Church and State in England,* Dr. Cyril Garbett, then Archbishop of York, stated that "except possibly in the early days, the Church of England never has had complete freedom. In the Middle Ages it was controlled by the Pope and the Crown; later by the Crown, and eventually by Parliament."[1] The most liberal interpretation of the term "religious freedom" can hardly encompass a situation in which a government prohibits a church from praying out of the prayer book the church wishes to use. Government dictation of how God is to be worshiped cannot be equated with religious liberty, even by the most ardent supporter of establishmentarianism.*

Yet that is exactly what happened in England in 1927 and 1928. In each of those years a proposal to revise the Anglican Prayer Book was rejected by a Parliament in which a majority were not members of the Anglican Church, and many of whom were Catholics, Jews, and even non-believers. The first measure was passed by the House of Lords, but both were rejected by the House of Commons. For fourteen years the church had been engaged in revising its prayer books; the proposed revision had been accepted by large majorities in the House of Bishops, the House of Clergy, and the House of Laity. In 1927 it took the House of Commons but a few hours to dispose of this work of fourteen years. In 1928 Parliament was more charitable, and devoted two full days to debate the issue; but the result

---

[1] Cyril Garbett, *Church and State in England* (Mystic, Conn.: Lawrence Verry, Inc., 1950), p. 5.

* "Establishmentarianism" refers to the doctrine that a particular religious denomination should have the support and official recognition of the state.

was the same. In the words of Archbishop Garbett, "Parliament refused legal authority to the Church to worship God in the manner its bishops, clergy and laity thought most fitting."[2] A commission of the Church of England summed up the situation neatly when it said that the rejection of the prayer book "revealed in unmistakable fashion the subordination of the Church to a Parliament which might consist largely of non-Christians, and does consist largely of persons who are not members of the Church of England."[3]

When Parliament was considering the proposed revision of the prayer book, Dr. Garbett was a young man, and upon being asked by the then Archbishop of Canterbury what action the Church should take if the proposal were rejected, he answered with the courage of youth, "we should ask for disestablishment." Twenty-five years later, when he was older, wiser, and the Archbishop of York, he believed disestablishment would be interpreted by the world "as the national repudiation of Christianity," and therefore opposed it.[4] A special commission set up by the church in 1949 to propose changes in the existing relationship between the church and the state reached the same conclusion. In January of 1952 it recommended that the church should have more freedom (as does the established Presbyterian Church in Scotland), but felt that "the unique relationship between Church and State in England is regarded by the world as a sign that the country has preserved a continuous Christian tradition," and that if "this relationship were broken it would be considered as a sign that England had abandoned Christianity."[5] *The Christian Century* commented on this that it would be hard to find a better example of the presumptuous nonsense on which much modern arguments for the principle of state churches rests.[6]

Occasional demands for disestablishment continue to be heard today, both within and without the Angelican Church. In 1955, Parliament rejected a motion by some Labour members that a royal commission be appointed to examine the question of separating the Church of England from the state. A similar motion was made in 1961, and again rejected. Within the church, suggestions for disestablishment continue to be opposed on the ground that it might be

---

[2] *Ibid.*, pp. 119–120.
[3] *Church and State*, Report of the Archbishop's Commission on the Relations between Church and State (1935) I, p. 41.
[4] Garbett, p. 146.
[5] *Religious News Service* (January 25, 1952).
[6] *The Christian Century* (February 13, 1952), 180.

construed as a repudiation of Christianity and lead to secularization of the state.

Disestablishment might or might not be construed as a repudiation of Christianity, but there can be no question that it would mean the loss by the church of certain tangible benefits which can hardly be considered unsubstantial. Under the establishment, the Church of England enjoys material advantages. First is the prestige which comes with being the national church. The reigning monarch must be a member of that church, and is crowned by the Archbishop of Canterbury. Secondly, the church as such participates in the governing of the country. The two archbishops and twenty-four bishops sit in the House of Lords as regular voting members, a privilege not accorded to the churchmen of any other religious denomination. Third, the duly rendered sentences of the ecclesiastical courts are enforced by the state, even to the extent of imprisoning those who disobey its lawfully issued judgments. Finally, under the establishment, the church enjoys properties and endowments amounting to several million pounds annually, which it would unquestionably lose on disestablishment.

But for these benefits the church pays dearly. The coin of payment is freedom, and the price is state control. The crown appoints all bishops and deans; and all bishops, incumbents, and curates must take an oath of allegiance to the crown before their consecration or ordination. No changes may be made legally in the doctrine or public worship of the church without an act of Parliament, with the result that Anglicans must choose between praying in a manner not consistent with church doctrine or clandestinely violate the laws.[7] In July 1964, the church had to apply to Parliament for the enactment of a measure permitting the clergy to wear ritual vestments at Holy Communion services. (Translate that into our terms, and imagine an America in which the change of the mass promulgated at Vatican II Council could not be effected without an act of Congress.) The convocations may meet only when summoned to do so by royal writ. The final court of appeal in ecclesiastical matters is a secular court. And lastly, the state exercises considerable control over the property and administration of the church.

The price for governmental aid is paid in Britain not only by the Anglican Church but by the other denominations which, though not the established church, nevertheless receive such aid. Roman Catholic schools, like Anglican, are financed out of tax-raised funds, but

---

[7] *Religious News Service* (July 9 and December 21, 1962).

in return are subject to strict supervision and control by the local public authorities. What this can lead to is indicated by the fact that in 1962 the Roman Catholic School of St. Mary and St. John in Wolverhampton found itself saddled with a local Communist Party official on its board of management. This situation is not uncommon in Communist countries, but few non-Communists claim that religious freedom prevails in these countries.

The Scandinavian Countries

When Protestants raise the cry of religious persecution in Spain, Catholics frequently counter with "What about Scandinavia?" Though the situations are far from equal—a Catholic church, for instance, need not conceal its identity in any Scandinavian country—there is nevertheless much validity to the countercharge. Protestants cannot in good faith assert that complete or substantially complete religious freedom prevails today in the Scandinavian countries, particularly in Sweden. All that can be said is that the restrictions on non-Lutherans are much less severe today than before January 1, 1952, the effective date of Sweden's first freedom of religion law since the establishment of the Lutheran Church in the sixteenth century.

Under the Swedish constitution the king and all his ministers must belong to the Lutheran Church, although the 1951 law amended the constitution so as to eliminate the religious test for members of the government. Freedom from constraint is assured to everyone "in the free exercise of his religion, provided he does not disturb public order or occasion general offense." Under the constitution, the king appoints the archbishops and bishops from among three persons nominated by the church for each vacancy. A general assembly of the church is provided for, to be convened by the king and to consider business which he presents. Decisions of the general assembly are merely petitions to the king and parliament, and have no effect until approved by them, though the general assembly may veto religious bills passed by parliament.

Religious instruction is compulsory in elementary, secondary, and teacher-training schools, although in recent years efforts have been made by governmental authorities to de-emphasize school prayers and substitute "objective" for doctrinal teaching of religion. If parents who are not members of the state church do not wish to have their children taught the Lutheran faith, they may have their children excused if they can demonstrate to the school board that they provide adequate religious training. Catholic Church spokesmen in this country, however, have complained that university admission officers do not give credit for non-Lutheran religious education.

Since January 1, 1952, a person born into the state church may leave it without having to join any other denomination, thus nullifying an 1873 law which required everyone to belong to some religious body. Children automatically become members of the state church at birth if either of their parents is a member, but after reaching eighteen any person may file in his registrar's office notice of intention to leave the church. Persons not belonging to the state church are relieved of paying one-half the church fees now imposed to cover the civic work of the clergy. The new law eliminated the requirement of membership in the state church for the holding of public office. It recognizes marriages performed by non-Lutheran clergy as having the same legal status as state church or civil marriages. Under the law, convents and monasteries may be established, for the first time since the Reformation, though government approval is still required in each case.

Few persons, perhaps not much more than 1 per cent of the population, have availed themselves of the opportunity to leave the Lutheran Church. The result is that practically all non-Catholic and non-Jewish children born in Sweden become members of the church and are required to participate in prayers and religious instruction in the public schools. Despite this only about 3 per cent attend religious services regularly, although most are married, have their children christened, and are buried by the church; or, as has been somewhat irreverently remarked, their contact with the church during their lives is limited to the times that they are hatched, matched, and dispatched.

In Norway and Denmark, as in Sweden, the Lutheran Church is established as the state church, and is both supported and controlled by the state. The king appoints the bishops and other high church officers. Freedom of worship is granted to non-Lutherans, but until 1956 Jesuits were excluded from Norway. In that year, Article 2 of the Norway constitution, which provided:

> The Evangelical-Lutheran religion shall remain the public religion of the State. The inhabitants professing it shall be bound to bring up their children in the same. Jesuits shall not be tolerated.

was amended to delete the last sentence.

Article VII of the Danish constitution reads:

The constitution of the Established Church shall be laid down by law.

The citizens shall have a right to join together in communities to worship God in the way that is in accordance with their convictions, provided that nothing is taught or done that is at variance with good morals or public order.

No person is bound to make personal contributions to any religious community other than the one to which he or she belongs.

The details of the religious communities other than the Established Church shall be regulated by law.

No person shall, on account of his or her religious belief, be excluded from the full enjoyment and privilege of civil and political rights or evade the fulfillment of any common duty as a citizen.

Religious instruction is obligatory in the schools of both Norway and Denmark, with a partial exemption to non-Lutheran children, who are excused from classes in dogma, but not Bible or church history. All teachers giving religious instruction must be approved by the bishop, and since most teachers do give such instructions, the practical effect is to close the teaching staff to non-Lutherans.

Other West European Countries

The relationship between religion and the state prevailing in France closely approximates that prevailing in the United States. Ever since 1905 there has been practically complete separation of church and state, together with full freedom to all religions. The first article of the French constitution states simply, "France is a republic, indivisible, secular, democratic and social." The preamble to the constitution provides that "The establishment of free, secular, public education on all levels is a duty of the State."

Consistent with this declaration, the French government is neutral to all religions and allows complete freedom to all. The public schools are entirely secular, and devoid of all religious instruction or exercises. In this respect France goes further than probably any other country, including most American states. It does not even permit members of religious orders to teach in the public schools. Since the question whether nuns and brothers may teach in the American public schools is a subject of considerable controversy in this country, it is appropriate to quote here the justification for this prohibition expressed by a French educational administrator:

Considerations of two kinds have influenced Parliament to exclude members of congregations from teaching. In the first place laicity of courses of study implies laicity of staffs. "The mission which the sectarian teachers believe themselves called upon to fulfill, the vows they have uttered, compel them to give the first place to the teaching of their religion." (Report to the Chamber of Deputies.) Added to this fact is another of a legal nature. The State cannot maintain in its civil hierarchy functionaries belonging to another hierarchy independent of it, to which they owe absolute obedience in all their actions. It can no more put up with this in education than it could in the army, for example, or in law.[8]

As in the United States, the church is free to establish parochial schools as long as they maintain minimum secular requirements. Until 1951 these schools received no financial support from the government, either directly or indirectly. In that year, however, after a bitter political controversy, two bills were adopted to provide some financial aid to the impoverished Catholic school system. One bill gave indirect aid by making state scholarships available to students in Catholic schools, while the other provided for financial allotments to Catholic parents' associations for educational purposes. In 1959 aid was further extended by enactment, after considerable controversy, of a bill providing for payment of teachers' salaries in private schools which undertook to admit "all children, regardless of origins, opinions and beliefs" and give them instruction "with full respect for freedom of conscience."

Belgium couples a constitutional guaranty of religious liberty to all with a grant of substantial government aid to the churches. Article 117 of the constitution provides that "the salaries and pensions of the ministers of religion shall be paid by the State." Under an agreement with the Catholic school authorities entered into in 1958, and a law enacted the next year to carry out the agreement, two hours of religious or moral instruction is required in all public schools, and the teachers must be approved by ecclesiastical authorities. The law also gives parents the right to request and obtain a new school, public or parochial, if they do not live reasonably close to the type of school they desire. The government pays teachers' salaries in all schools, but pays only for the buildings of the public schools. While the privilege of maintaining government-supported religious schools is available to all denominations, the Catholic Church is, with slight exceptions, the only one to exercise it.

The Netherlands constitution likewise provides for religious freedom and equality, with provision for public aid to the various

---

[8] M. Searle Bates, *Religious Liberty: An Inquiry* (New York: International Missionary Council, 1945), p. 343.

sects. The constitution imposes on the state the obligation to pay adequate salaries to all ministers of religion.

For almost half of a century, ever since 1920, the Netherlands has provided public support for confessional schools equally with public schools. In view of the contention frequently made by Catholic sources in this country that the Netherlands' adjustment of the claims of the church schools on the state treasury is a fair solution of the problem that might well be emulated here, it may be well to examine the effect of the government's action of the Netherlands' public school system. In 1850, of students enrolled in the primary schools, 77 per cent were in the public schools and 23 per cent in the private schools. In 1958 the percentages were almost exactly reversed —28 per cent in the public schools and 72 per cent in the private schools.

According to Theodore L. Reller, dean of the school of education at the University of California at Berkeley, who has made a special study of the situation in Holland, the division of tax-raised funds between public and confessional schools has resulted in a segmented society. It has also adversely affected education. Surprisingly, rather than achieving diversity and experimentation, the pursuit of equality in government support has resulted in standardization and in uniformity and in lack of initiative by public and private schools and by the municipalities. Public schools find it difficult to move because the municipality constantly notes that anything done for any public school must be provided in all private schools on request.[9]

Moreover, because of the limited perspectives of the confessional schools, social sciences are taught inadequately. Each religious school system teaches the facts of history strictly from its own view. There is practically no cooperation among teachers or schools in the development of common understanding. Each group lives within its own circle. When teachers of different schools meet, they discuss only technical matters such as salaries, technical aids, etc. All in all, Dean Reller concludes that the Dutch system is not one to be emulated in the United States.

Switzerland presents a variety of church-state arrangements among its many cantons. Some have one established church, some two, some three, and some none. The present trend seems to be toward separation. The relationships in the cantons are, however, sub-

---

[9] Theodore L. Reller, "Public Funds for Religious Education," in Donald A. Gianella (ed.), *Religion and the Public Order, 1964* (Chicago: University of Chicago Press, 1965), p. 187.

ject to the limitations of the federal constitution, which guarantees freedom of conscience, requires that the "public schools shall be such that they may be frequented by adherents of all religious confessions," prohibits taxing any person for the specific benefit of a church to which he does not belong, and bars entry of the Jesuit order in the country, though individual Jesuits are at liberty to engage in their work.

West Germany ("The Federal Republic of Germany") adopted a constitution in 1949. Before that, relations between the churches and the states or *Länder* were principally a matter for determination by each state. Relations with the Catholic Church were governed by concordats entered into with the Vatican. Under these concordats the states, while guaranteeing freedom of religion and self-administration, undertook to contribute to the upkeep of the diocese, whose property was made free from taxation, to maintain religious instruction in schools under church supervision, and to provide theological training in the universities. For its part, the church acknowledged the right of the states to pass on church appointments. These concordats were not affected by the 1949 constitution and are still effective.

In addition to these separate concordats, the Vatican entered into a concordat with Adolph Hitler in 1933 under which the Nazi government agreed to pay the salaries of some of the Catholic clergy, permit religious orders to establish schools freely and with rights equal to those of equivalent state institutions, allow freedom of communication between the Pope and the German bishops, and permit Catholics in youth organizations the opportunity to perform their religious duties. According to Vatican sources, this concordat created a moral and legal obligation which remains binding on the new West German government. In 1957, the Constitutional Court agreed that the 1933 concordat was still valid and binding upon the West German government, but because of the independence of the *Länder* they could not be compelled to support Catholic institutions and schools.

The Lutheran and Reformed churches in the states are subject to state supervision and receive state subsidies. They enjoy the right to levy church taxes on their members, which are collected by the state. The Methodists and the Baptists, though entitled to the same privilege, prefer to do their own collecting, but the Jews have regularly levied church taxes.

Because of the close relation of church and state in Germany, church influence on education was strong even under the Nazis. Generally speaking, three types of schools developed: (1) The secular school, which was legally exempt from including religion in the course of study. No pupil could be required to take part in religious instruction unless his parents consented. (2) The interdenominational school, which divided children along denominational lines for religious instruction. Class work in other subjects was given to all pupils in common. (3) The denominational school, which included only teachers and pupils of the same religious confession.

These relations continue substantially unchanged under the new constitution. This constitution guarantees freedom of faith and conscience, including the right to refrain from combatant war service for reasons of conscience (Article 4). Article 7 places the entire education system under state supervision, with the right in the parents to determine whether their children shall receive religious instruction, which is made part of the curriculum of the state schools. No teacher in the state schools may be required to give religious instructions against his will, and the right to establish private schools is guaranteed.

. . . .

Summary*

A number of conclusions can reasonably be drawn from this brief summary of contemporary solutions to the problem of reconciling the rival claims of church and state:

(1) Religious liberty is generally most secure where church and state are most completely separated. Conversely, religious liberty suffers where the state seeks to make the church an engine to further national policy, or the church seeks to utilize the compulsive arm of the state to further religious interests.

(2) This proposition is true not only in totalitarian countries, but to a lesser extent in democracies as well.

(3) Anti-religious and atheistic government finds little difficulty in entering into alliances with churches.

(4) A church receiving special state favors invariably pays for them in the loss of religious freedom.

---

* Some of the earlier passages summarized here have been deleted from this reprinting of Pfeffer's discussion.

(5) Revolutionary governments of countries in which the churches were politically powerful and aligned with the exploiting classes exhibit strong anti-religious tendencies and impose severe restrictions on religious liberty.

(6) The newer democracies have been greatly influenced by the American experiment, and make constitutional provision for complete religious liberty and the separation of church and state.

Chapter Two

The Unique American Experience— Early Development

As the preceding exposition by Leo Pfeffer makes clear, each country has handled the relationship of religion to the state in its own more or less distinctive manner, as dictated by its particular history and institutions. The early development of religion in the American colonies was unique because the country was settled largely by people who had emigrated for a variety of strong religious reasons. Unlike their contemporary European revolutionaries, who considered religion the enemy of political change, the founders of the United States tended to equate multi-denominational Christianity with the revolutionary ideals of justice and equality.

The result of this early predisposition has been not only a relatively high mutual tolerance among the different religious sects in this country, but a widespread belief in the positive social value of church-going and moral utterance. Despite periods of unreasoned anti-Catholicism and anti-Semitism, the principal sufferers from American religious ideology have been the non-believers. In continental European countries (with their strong anti-clerical movements) agnosticism and atheism can be freely espoused and debated, but the tolerance of the American public for open non-belief has been quite low. Probably because of the assumed relationship between religion and the "American way of life," the non-believer is commonly castigated as "un-American" and classified with whatever foreign enemy seems most dangerous to the "American way" at any given time in history. Even the Supreme Court has been accused, in the after-

math of its decision forbidding religious devotions in public schools, of contributing to "godlessness in America" and thus preparing the way for a
Communist takeover.*

The following selections will provide an historical perspective on the
development of religion in the United States, both as institution apart from
government and as an integral contributor to the moral base of American democratic assumptions.

The Background of American Religious Freedom†

Anson P. Stokes and Leo Pfeffer

The Threefold Colonial Tradition

The ultimate roots of American Church–State separation and
religious freedom are, of course, to be found in the history of the
Old World. Major Old-World influences include the Decalogue, which
provided the basis of the moral law of Israel and in a later simplified
form of Christianity; the Greek city-states, and especially Athens,
which must be mentioned among the historic precursors of American
democracy; the philosophers who lived in and inspired the lives of
these city-states; the teachings of Christianity; the Roman Empire
and its religions; the Catholic Church and its doctrines and practices;
and the Renaissance and the Reformation which it made possible.
Of the two greatest leaders of the Reformation, Martin Luther and
John Calvin, the latter had the deeper influence on political organization and religious thought in the United States. It was his views
that largely molded the thinking of the Congregationalists of New
England and the Scotch Presbyterians, together with the closely
related Dutch Reformed Church, of the middle states, and even of
the Anglicans in the South.

---

* The connection between American anti-communism and fundamentalist religion is a central concern of another Insight Series book, *Protest from the Right*,
by Robert Rosenstone.

† From *Church and State in the United States* by Anson Phelps Stokes and
Leo Pfeffer; copyright © 1950, 1964 by Estate of Anson Phelps Stokes and by
Leo Pfeffer; reprinted with the permission of Harper & Row, Publishers, Inc.,
New York; (Evanston, Ill.: Harper and Row, 1950), pp. 3–9, 21–27, 36–40.

A vital role was played, too, by the Anabaptists and other despised and persecuted Christian sects originating in Central Europe in the second quarter of the sixteenth century. By upholding their right to religious freedom based on Biblical and Reformation teachings, they paved the way, through the Baptists, Quakers, and others, for our American religious freedom. Among the strongest promoters of religious freedom were the Socinians of the sixteenth century, later to be called Unitarians. But of the religious groups it was the Independents or Separatists who made the greatest contribution to civil liberty, education, and democratic polity in the United States.

Various provisions of the English constitution—some embodied in statutes, others in unwritten laws and customs—had direct impact on the development of the ideas of liberty in the American frame of government. Among these should be mentioned the Magna Charta, the Bill of Rights of 1689, and the Acts of Toleration of 1689 and 1693.

The thinking of Thomas Jefferson and other founders of the American republic was greatly influenced, too, by a group of seventeenth- and eighteenth-century philosophers on the European continent and in England: Charles Louis Montesquieu, a believer in a written constitution, whose *L'esprit des lois* appeared in 1748 with its comparative study of the ideas of a republic, a monarchy, and a despotism; Jean Jacques Rousseau, whose *Contrat social*, with its theory of popular sovereignty and the need of full citizenship for the complete development of manhood, appeared in 1762; and François Marie de Voltaire, who strongly opposed any State Church with exclusive rights and privileges and pleaded for full religious freedom.

However, it was the Englishman John Locke who of all modern philosophers carried the most weight among statesmen such as Thomas Jefferson and James Madison, who in turn laid the framework of our civil and religious liberties. He taught that the magistrate had no authority to rule over souls; that religion must depend on inward conviction, not on external compulsion; and that the rights of conscience in matters of personal religious faith must be treated with respect. He believed in government by consent and maintained that liberty, life, and property or "estate" were inalienable rights, inherent in or natural to every individual, and thus antedated government.[1]

These, then, were some of the major intellectual and spiritual Old World forces, religious and non-religious, that helped shape

---

[1] See particularly John Locke, *Letter Concerning Toleration.*

American concepts of democracy, religious freedom, and Church–State relationships. But the more immediate influences must be sought in the New World and particularly in the threefold colonial tradition in what was to become the United States.

Although Church–State conditions in colonial times varied with the type of colony, in general the colonies largely reflected the spirit of the home government at the time, as far as toleration was concerned. More specifically, the relation between Church and State, and the resulting degree of religious freedom, developed along three independent though parallel lines: in Puritan New England, in Anglican Virginia and some other Southern colonies, and in the proprietary middle and Southern colonies.

The Pilgrims of Plymouth and the Puritans of Massachusetts Bay had all been originally Puritans—men who wished to purify the Church of England. After about two generations of separate existence in New England, the Puritans, who had always been nonconformists but had also become Separatists as far as the Church of England was concerned, again absorbed their more liberal-minded Separatist brethren of Plymouth. This occurred in 1692 when Plymouth and Massachusetts were united under a new charter. Before that, however, although they were almost all Calvinists, there were distinct differences among the members of the two groups.

In Plymouth, which was definitely more liberal and less theocratic* than Massachusetts Bay, the seal of effective authority was in the rank and file of yeomen rather than, as in Massachusetts Bay, in the magistrates and ministers. The Pilgrims repudiated the Church of England but recognized their allegiance to the king, while the Puritans, desiring to build a State without a king, rejected the royal authority as much as they dared but recognized their fealty to the English Church in all things spiritual. The Pilgrims differed most from the Puritans in their more democratic spirit, as may be seen from the Mayflower Compact of 1620, with its acceptance of the principle of majority rule. Because of the inability of the Plymouth colonists to secure a charter from the home government, this Compact virtually served them as their constitution.

The democratic spirit prevailing at Plymouth is indicated by the fact that in the early years legislation was shared by all freemen, although later it was vested in an elected governor and General Court. Not to accept election when first chosen to office was a serious, punishable offense.

---

* "Theocracy" is government of the state by church leaders.

THE UNIQUE AMERICAN EXPERIENCE — EARLY DEVELOPMENT 19

However, it was not Plymouth but Massachusetts Bay, with Boston as the principal port of entry into New England, that became the colony destined to develop Puritanism in its most influential form and to place its mark on the United States more than any colony other than Virginia (which led in the making of political constitutions). Here religion, of an intolerant Calvinistic type, and government were to be closely associated in accordance with English tradition; a Puritan State Church, especially closely related to town government, gradually developed from non-conformity to take the place of the old Anglican State Church to which the Puritans had been accustomed in England. The Church was a carefully selected group of communicants who emphasized their prerogatives and would brook no serious dissent from their duly adopted tenets. They expected the State to support public worship and suppress heresy. They did not wish it to interfere in strictly religious questions but recognized that in matters of Church government and ecclesiastical affairs State and Church should work together.

In New England, the (Congregational) meetinghouse, the nucleus of every township, was used both for governmental purposes and for religious worship. Furthermore, municipal and certain parochial duties were frequently performed by the same officials. In some cases the minutes of the two organizations were kept in the same book, the facts and votes of both groups being included. Yet, even in Puritan New England, a fairly clear distinction was maintained between the functions of Church and State. For example, the elder was not considered eligible for the civil magistracy nor the magistrate for the office of elder. The two functions were considered separate.

During most of the colonial period Congregationalism was the Established Church in New England, outside of Rhode Island. It received all taxes for the support of religion, although, under certain conditions in the later period, the individual taxpayer might designate that his taxes be assigned to another publicly recognized religious group.

It was only as the early settlers died off and with the decrease of emphasis on church membership—based on religious experience, the usual test of suffrage among the freemen—that the voting privilege was extended and that both Church and State became more democratic. Before that time there was a close connection between the two "powers" in New England, especially in Massachusetts. When Anne Hutchinson was put out of the church in Boston the action was taken first by the church and subsequently by the magistrate; when the first council or synod was held in New England, it was attended not only by twenty-three ministers from Massachusetts and two from Connecticut, but by the body of the magistrates, and its expenses were met out of the general colonial treasury. The governor and his assistants in Massachusetts Bay were frequently referred to as "the nursing fathers of the churches," for they concerned themselves with diverse matters involving congregational life, doctrine, and policy and played a major part in determining certain church matters, such as where new arrivals among the clergy should be assigned. They even called synods of the church and ordered ministers to formulate a confession of faith and a form of discipline.

The influence of the clergy in New England was undoubtedly very large. The ministers, however, generally refrained from accepting important political office and had to bow to the civil authorities in many Church matters. They were content so long as the State was administered by sympathetic members of their Church but bitterly opposed the entire separation of Congregationalism from the State in its two great strongholds, Massachusetts and Connecticut. In the early days, especially in Massachusetts Bay, Quakers, Baptists, and other dissenting groups were outrageously treated, but no more so than in England at the same time.

In Connecticut, the general Church–State setup was about the same as in Massachusetts. The fact is that outside of Rhode Island, where two groups of Independents—Baptists and Quakers—were powerful, and where Roger Williams and John Clarke proved great leaders in behalf of entire separation of Church and State, very little was accomplished in the way of religious freedom as distinct from toleration until the period of the American Revolution.

As Puritanism dominated New England, so Anglicanism dominated Virginia and the other Southern colonies. It was at Jamestown in Virginia that the Anglican–Protestant tradition was legally recognized when the first representative body of legislators to meet in North America, assembling in 1619 in their place of worship, established the authority of the Church of England and took measures for its support. In a word, the Anglican Church became a State Church in Virginia, much as the Puritan Church was somewhat later established in Massachusetts, but with this difference: in Virginia the State controlled the Church; in Massachusetts the Church tended to control the State. In Virginia in the seventeenth century the governor, within his limited sphere, executed the ecclesiastical prerogatives of the crown and, in the absence of a resident bishop, assumed a quasi-episcopal direction of the clergy. His instructions and colonial statutes recognized the exclusive claims of the Church of England. This condition lasted until the Revolutionary period. Even then the leaders of the state favored the government's retaining a definite relationship to religion and education, which would mean in most communities that the Episcopal Church would continue to be responsible for the latter.

In general the Southern colonies had an official tie-up with the Anglican Church much as most of the New England colonies had with the Congregational churches. However, the seat of authority for Anglicanism was in England; for Puritanism, in New England. New England's official religion was mainly master of its own destinies; in the South official religion was not. So in the colonial period the Northern clergy developed more leadership and more influence on State policy than did their Southern colleagues. Furthermore, the clergy in the Southern colonies, being by church tradition dependent on Episcopal supervision but having none except that of the distant Bishop of London, were frequently disloyal to their trust as spiritual and moral leaders, thereby helping to bring about disestablishment in Virginia about half a century before it took place in Connecticut and Massachusetts.

The proprietary middle and Southern provinces—New York (including originally New Jersey and Delaware), the Carolinas, Pennsylvania, and Maryland—provided more of a melting pot of religious and national groups than any other part of America and consequently were generally ahead of other sections in developing religious freedom. Moreover, we find here a semifeudal association of government with land ownership, where the proprietors' prosperity depended upon the steady flow of immigration. In these colonies or provinces, consequently, a practical type of liberalism prevailed in welcoming newcomers of various types, although Quakers dominated in Pennsylvania; Roman Catholics, followed by Anglicans, in Maryland; and Presbyterians and Quakers, following Anglicans, in New Jersey. The Dutch Reformed and Anglicans sought mastery in New York, where, in spite of alternating Dutch and English rule, there was more tolerance than in New England.

An early example was the attitude of the town of Flushing, Long Island, many of whose freemen, incensed by Governor Peter Stuyvesant's banning of the Quakers in 1657 in spite of the provisions of their town charter of 1645 guaranteeing "the right to have and

enjoy liberty of conscience," drew up the "Flushing Remonstrance."
In this they proclaimed that they would welcome not only members
of this sect but any "sons of Adam who came in love among us,"
and would not "condemn, punish, banish, prosecute or lay violent
hands upon anyone, in whatever name, form or title he might
appear." We are, therefore, not surprised to find that in the middle
of the eighteenth century the spirit of toleration had so developed—
howbeit largely for prudential rather than for ideological or ideal-
istic reasons—that the advertisement regarding the opening of
King's (Columbia) College in New York in 1754 read, "there is no
intention to impose on the scholars the peculiar tenets of any particular sect of Christians, but to inculcate upon their tender minds,
the great Principles of Christianity and Morality, in which true
Christians of each Denomination are generally agreed."[2] Similar
ideals prevailed at about the same time at the leading institution
of learning in another one of the middle colonies—what is now the
University of Pennsylvania.

Conditions in New Jersey were not dissimilar to those in New
York, with which it was generally associated, sharing the alternating
Dutch and English supremacy. In 1677 "West Jersey" came under
William Penn's control, and his "Concessions and Agreements of the
Proprietors, Freeholders and Inhabitants" assured religious tolera-
tion, a relatively large portion of which continued after the provinces
were transferred to the crown of England.

Penn's efforts for religious freedom in Pennsylvania were particularly notable. Indeed, only here, in Delaware—which was originally part of the province—and in Rhode Island do we find "free
colonies" with substantial liberty of conscience for non-Christians
and without any established Church. Even in Pennsylvania, however,
religious tests, in spite of the absence of an establishment, were of
a rather narrow Protestant type. But for its day the attitude was
relatively liberal, owing mainly to Penn's "Frame of Government"
of 1683, which welcomed to full rights all citizens "who profess to
believe in Jesus Christ."

As early as 1700, the General Assembly of Delaware enacted a
law granting full liberty of conscience to any person professing
belief in Almighty God. In Carolina considerable liberty of conscience was promised to all Protestant dissenters who emigrated to
the colony, and in Maryland a special act tolerating all Trinitarian
Christians was passed by the Assembly in 1649.

---

[2] Conrad H. Moehlman, *School and Church*, p. 26.

In respect to the proprietary colonies it may be said that in general not only did the proprietors, eager to advance the economic prosperity of territories under their control by securing more settlers, let down theological and ecclesiastical bars but the Quaker influence centering in Pennsylvania stood in the main for freedom. Furthermore, in the period from 1660 to 1775 when the proprietary colonies were being developed with such enthusiasm, the colonial population was being increased by over two million people—an increase largely due to this new type of land-grant colony. The new settlers were generally attracted by the religious freedom offered and were determined to continue and develop it.

.   .   .   .

The Colonists' Migrations and Resulting Divergent Sects

There were undoubtedly many factors which encouraged early American settlement. Some modern historians have emphasized the economic note, that is, the colonists' desire for improving financial conditions, and especially for securing land of their own. Others have been impressed with the struggle for national ascendance in America because of its effect on the balance of power in Europe, especially the curbing of Catholic Spain and France—a movement encouraged by the British government. Still others call attention to the desire of large groups of middle-class people to get away from conservative restraints and to improve their social status by leaving countries where class lines were still fairly rigid. The reasons for making the long journey were indeed many and varied. Some Europeans yielded to their love of change and adventure, generally because a new world meant to them a new economic opportunity (available good land in the old countries was scarce) ; some hoped to escape political oppression, including some of the burdens of supporting reactionary governments in the old lands, with heavy taxes, military service, and other obligations.

These and other factors, social, economic, political, all played their part. Yet the fact remains that the religious factor, at one time so exclusively emphasized and so exaggerated as to produce a reaction, is beginning again to receive due attention : One of the prime causes for early migration to America, and especially to New England, was the desire for religious freedom.

This does not mean that there were many among the colonists who held convictions as to the rightness of religious freedom per se, but rather that they wished to escape from what they believed to be ecclesiastical tyranny, as far as the treatment of their own sect or denomination was concerned. Members of various Protestant groups wished to avoid persecution or hampering regulations for themselves; yet they might be found to turn around on arrival in America and persecute their old enemies or opponents, whether these were Roman Catholics, Anglicans, or adherents of some dominantly Calvinist body. There were also group migrations based on common religious bonds where some non-conformists, such as the Mennonites, came over in communities so as to have freedom to develop their own religious and social convictions. Religious freedom in America had its roots three hundred years ago in the desire of tens of thousands of settlers to free themselves and the religious group to which they belonged from State interference with their development. This factor also played an important part in twentieth-century immigration, especially on the part of the Jews of Eastern Europe and the people of Ireland, cases in which economic, religious, and political elements were all combined.

The founders of the American colonies were, relatively speaking, largely political liberals and religious non-conformists, at least insofar as dissatisfaction with European conditions was concerned. This was true not only of the early English immigration but even more so of the West European migration which followed in 1660 and included so many German sectaries with Anabaptist backgrounds— Mennonites, Moravians, Quakers, and so on. Different colonies also had their distinctive religious and ecclesiastical flavors due to the dominant points of view, such as that of the Puritans in Massachusetts or of the Anglicans in Virginia; but there were probably more different religious backgrounds than have been generally recognized. Hence the existence of elements in the colonies which in time would oppose the historic union of Church and State and advocate religious freedom. There were a few such liberals even in Massachusetts; but most of the very pronounced ones migrated to Rhode Island, where they had entire freedom of conscience, or to some of the middle colonies, such as Pennsylvania, where they had it in large measure.

Calvinism, with the "infallible" Bible which the colonists carried with them, was too firmly entrenched, especially in New England, for liberalism to show itself prominently in the field of theology. But the Calvinists were separated by three thousand miles of sea from the center of government, and communication was irregular and slow. It was inevitable that they would break away from the conservative tradition of government to which they had been accustomed, and from whose extremes they had fled, to try something new, although they would not depart from Calvin's principle of some partnership between Church and State. The simple character of colonial life in most sections outside of the few large towns and the plantation South added its influence, as did the democratic ideal of brotherhood in the New Testament.

The fact that immigration to the United States in the colonial period and the period when our government was being formed was mainly English was of great importance from the standpoint of religious freedom; for although England retained a State Church she increasingly, after the Revolution of 1688 and the issuance the following year of the Act of Tolerance, practiced a considerable measure of toleration. When we compare the conditions in England, for instance, with those in the Latin countries of Europe up to the time of the French Revolution, we can see how much more freedom came to America as a result of our Anglo-Saxon tradition than would have come had our tradition been dominantly Latin.

The factor of experience of European persecution must also be taken into account as a stimulus to religious freedom in this country. People who have suffered for their views naturally want freedom to express them, and the large majority of pre-Revolutionary settlers in America—except in some parts of the South—had been members of reluctantly tolerated or actively persecuted groups abroad. A full list of these persecutions would be a large one, but for our purpose the important thing to remember is that the persecuted groups became to a large extent the leaders in behalf of religious freedom in the new land.

The variety of sects with differing European backgrounds that colonized America was a potent factor in bringing about religious freedom. The perpetual conflict among the sects was in the long run conductive to liberty. Some of the fathers of the Republic, such as Jefferson and Madison, realized this. Indeed, the idea goes back at least to Voltaire, who put the matter extremely and bluntly but with much truth in his *Lettres sur les Anglais*: "If there were one religion in England, its despotism would be terrible; if there were only two, they would destroy each other; but there are thirty, and therefore they live in peace and happiness."[3] Voltaire tells us that he based this conclusion, not on the natural tolerance of the English people, but on a study of intolerance of various groups, including Anglicans and Scotch Presbyterians.

---

[3] Cited by Francesco Ruffini, *Religious Liberty*, p. 295.

Small Percentage of Church Members in the Colonies

The Church leaders in the colonies, especially in early New England, took their religion so seriously that we are inclined to overestimate the Church devotion of the majority of the population. Even in the earliest days, a majority of the colonists, in spite of the religious objectives stated by their leaders, were probably actuated mainly by economic considerations. Earnest ministers and laymen gave a religious note to the early settlements. However, after the first generation with its heroic qualities died off, the impulse for converting the Indians waned, and ecclesiastical rigidity and arid theological controversy dried up the sources of religious vitality, the number of active church members was almost everywhere very small. A leading authority has estimated that at the close of the colonial period New England, the best-churched section of the thirteen colonies, had no more than one church member to every eight persons in the total population.[4] Another authority, writing of a slightly earlier period in New England—the end of the seventeenth century and the beginning of the eighteenth—does not think that over one out of twenty or twenty-five New Englanders belonged to the churches. In comparison with these figures, the *Yearbook of American Churches* for 1962 reported a total church membership in the United States of close to 115 million persons, or some 63.6 per cent of the nation's estimated population.[5]

These typical facts and figures are sufficient to show that non-church members at the time our state and national constitutions were being formed were in a large majority, and that it was quite natural for them to oppose any organic connection between Church and State.

Experience With and Without Establishments

Nothing had a larger effect on the framers of our Constitution and Bill of Rights than colonial experience as well as experience during the Revolutionary period, when the states were being formed. Most of the features of Church–State separation and of religious freedom can be traced back in the colonial period to the achievements of Roger Williams in Rhode Island and of William Penn in Pennsylvania, and in the state period to the achievements of Virginia and New York in securing virtually complete religious freedom and entire separation between Church and State. Furthermore, those colonies

---

[4] See W. W. Sweet, "Church Membership," *Dictionary of American History.*

[5] Harold E. Davis, "Religion, American," *Dictionary of American History.*

which had an Established Church, although that Church had much support from its adherents, had developed a strong opposition party, made up in the South of non-conformists, as far as Anglicanism was concerned, and in the North of non-conformists who opposed the special privileges of the Congregational establishment. It was clear to the great majority in the Constitutional Convention of 1787 not only that the federal government must have no Church connection but that such connection would gradually disappear in the various states, although the new government could not go too far or too fast in definitely aiding this movement.

Any impartial person who knew the conditions in an American colony with an Established Church well knew the difficulties. He might wish to maintain his Church in his own colony in spite of these, but when it came to legislating for the nation starting under a new republican form of government he could not but see the need of a change. In such states as Massachusetts with its entrenched Congregationalism there had been an increasingly persistent and bitter struggle. The "outs" were constantly agitating publicly and petitioning the legislatures to give up tithes and other forms of taxes for the support of the establishment, and to grant the people entire freedom before the law for their work. Indeed, in a good many cases that had come before the courts, individuals—often on conscientious grounds —had declined to suport the Established Church, and the dissenters were steadily increasing their demands. If such was the condition in a relatively homogeneous state, what would it be in the nation at large if an establishment of religion were attempted? It was quite obvious that, with all the extreme dissenting German sects in Pennsylvania, the Dutch Reformed and Presbyterians in New York, the Roman Catholics in Maryland, the Episcopalians in Virginia, the Quakers in Rhode Island, the Jews in a few cities like New York, Charleston, and Newport, and the vigorous Baptists expanding along the Appalachian frontier and stirring up trouble for establishments everywhere, a national State Church was out of the question.

Four of the original thirteen colonies had secured and experienced religious freedom with entire separation of Church and State and found that it actually worked well. The object lesson of Rhode Island's experiment in New England and the success of Pennsylvania, with its closely related Delaware, in the middle states, of Maryland's early efforts under Cecil Calvert, and of Virginia's recent victory in the South were bound to make the framers of the Constitution appreciate the importance of religious freedom and guard

against any federal Church for the United States. The founding
fathers sensed full well that any other solution would be inconsistent
with the principles of independence and democracy.

Effects of the Great Awakening

One very definite evangelical movement aided the cause of religious freedom just prior to the formation of the Union. This was
the Great Awakening in the middle of the eighteenth century. Its
origin was due to two major factors: the middle colonies revival,
which had its roots in German Pietism, and the New England
"awakening." The efforts of the leaders of the middle colonial revival
did much both for vital religion and for democracy, especially on the
frontier, and in some places, such as Virginia, contributed to over-
throwing the domination of the State Church. This result was due
partly to accessions to non-conformist strength and partly to the
breaking up of the old parish system with its one recognized minister
and church with responsibility for nearly all in the community.

The New England movement had its beginnings in 1734, a few
years after the onset of the revival in the middle colonies, but it was
probably even more influential and was identified with the name of
Jonathan Edwards, the greatest of the Puritans. A theologian and
a mystic, Edwards cared little about political matters. Yet he contributed mightily—even though indirectly, being far from a liberal
in theology—to the cause of religious freedom. He preached the
importance of individual conversion; he insisted that the Church and
the State were very different and that the Church should be exalted
as a spiritual and not a political institution; he effectively proclaimed
that each individual is answerable to God alone; and his strict
theological and ecclesiastical views alienated the more liberal, who
considered a moral life more important than Calvinistic orthodoxy
and so tended to leave established Congregationalism for other religious groups more sympathetic with their point of view. Edwards,
perhaps far beyond all men of his time, smote the staggering blow
which made ecclesiastical establishments impossible to America,
although it is unlikely that he meant to do anything of the kind.

The Great Awakening profoundly moved all Protestant groups
and prepared the soil for change. It affected the Anglicans by re-
actions from without rather than direct internal influence, in that
the extremes of the revival led many to seek the more restrained and
orderly worship of the Episcopal Church. It put new life in those
dissenting churches in New England, especially the Baptists, and
the Methodist group then included among the Episcopalians, upon

which the cause of religious liberty so much depended. In these churches the Awakening was considered a protest against the deadness of what was virtually State religion, corresponding in this respect to Pietism in Germany and Methodism in England. The stricter new standards strengthened the moral and religious tone of the established Congregational Church, which had been weakened by compromise, and girded it for new crusades. The Great Awakening was, on the whole, a severe blow to the cause of Church establishments.

The movement against slavery; the development of a humanitarian interest in many other causes; the bringing of men together in a common movement from different colonies and from different Protestant groups; the encouraging of democratic ideals; the providing of religion on the frontier; the founding of educational institutions such as Princeton College; and the strengthening of the Presbyterian, Baptist, Congregational, and other Churches, which contributed so much popular support to the cause of the American Revolution—these are among the direct and indirect historical influences of the Great Awakening on American civil and religious life.

As this movement had its effective beginnings in New England and has been largely discussed by New England authors, its influence on the South and West has not always been adequately realized. It was, however, demonstrably a mighty force in other distant colonies. For instance, in Virginia it gave great stimulus through the Baptist and Presbyterian churches to the cause of civil and religious liberty. It aided these movements by pressure from below, opposing all monarchical forms of State and Church control and encouraging mightily the democratic movement.

Freemasonry

A large number of the leaders of the movement that resulted in the American Revolution and in the establishment of the American Constitution were Freemasons. These included James Otis, Benjamin Franklin, George Washington (who took his oath of office as president upon his Masonic Bible), as well as fourteen signers of the Declaration of Independence and many who were active in the Constitutional Convention. There were, however, some conspicuous exceptions: John Adams, Patrick Henry, and Thomas Jefferson. Possibly the secret aspects of Freemasonry made them feel that it was inadvisable to identify themselves with the movement.

Although the matter has been little referred to by American historians other than Masonic writers, it seems clear that the

Masonic lodges, which had been active for a generation prior to the Revolution, influenced not only the impulse toward the new republic but also the cause of religious toleration, and in several ways.

They brought together, through correspondence, visitation, conventions, encampments, and various other meetings, the Anglicans of the South, the Congregationalists of New England, the Presbyterians of the middle colonies, the Baptists, and other groups.

They established military lodges in the Revolutionary army which encouraged the same broadening of friendships and contacts.

They asserted their belief in "the great Architect of the universe" and yet took the ground that they would not identify themselves as an organization with any denomination.

They helped to develop a deep interest in the general cause of social welfare, with loyalty to both the moral and the spiritual ideals of the Bible and the Crusades, emphasis on self-government, and respect for differences of religious convictions and for honest craftsmanship in any occupation.

They encouraged a friendly attitude toward the Jews, for whose ancient standards of personal and public righteousness and for whose temple ceremonies, symbols, and mystic rites they had a profound respect. The Scottish Rite today includes many representative Jews in its membership.

They showed a sympathetic interest in the Negro, granting a warrant for the first colored lodge, in Boston, in 1784, and the first state grand lodge, in Massachusetts, in 1808.

They emphasized the idea which is at the basis of the Declaration of Independence: that the universe and all men in it are of divine origin, and that natural law demands the treatment of all men fairly in accordance with their origin and destiny.

They were naturally antagonistic to the Church–State idea, laying supreme emphasis on the individual's freedom of conscience.

.   .   .   .

[The National Tradition]

The actual situation in the states at the beginning of the national period made further guarantees of religious freedom essential. It is estimated that from 1776 to 1820 nearly 250,000 immigrants came to the United States. This influx, although small in comparison with the movement that set in after the War of 1812, was nonetheless highly significant from our standpoint, especially as it included a considerable number of Roman Catholics, some Jews, and representatives of many other religious groups from nearly all parts of Europe.

The realization grew that the United States, partly because it was a new country with vast resources, partly because of its democratic form of government, and partly because of hard conditions of life in certain European areas, would attract constantly increasing numbers of immigrants, and that they were needed for the development of the country. In view of the increasingly variegated character of its population, the nation must have religious freedom.

Turning from without to within, we find the situation equally significant. It was manifestly impossible under existing conditions to have a Federal Congregational Church, even should some extremists in New England want it, or a Federal Episcopal Church, even if some Southern Episcopalians had thought it desirable. The only way Congregationalists, Presbyterians, Baptists, and Episcopalians, the four largest colonial groups, in the order named, as well as Mennonites, Quakers, Dutch Reformed, Roman Catholics, Jews, Methodists, Lutherans, and others, could unite in forming a Federal government was on the basis of religious freedom.

It will be seen then, that, leaving out of account for the moment the influence of the theories of European and American philosophers and various historical factors, the actual, practical necessities of the situation at the end of the eighteenth century in the United States could not be met by a State Church or even by mere toleration on the part of the dominant Protestants of other religious groups. Complete religious freedom, as long as it did not involve acts contrary to the safety of the State or public morals, was clearly indicated as the only possible solution. The mere fact that new religious denominations could be established at will without government approval would of itself prevent much criticism by those dissatisfied with existing conditions and would tend to create a spirit of good will.

The Influence of the Churches During and Immediately After the Revolution

At the beginning of the American Revolution nine out of the thirteen colonies had an Established Church. During its course some progress was made in the direction of separation and religious freedom by the newly organized states. At its close, when the Constitutional Convention was meeting in Philadelphia in 1787, all the New England states except Rhode Island retained what was virtually established Congregationalism; Maryland and South Carolina continued their Church of England connection, which had just been given up by Virginia, North Carolina, and Georgia; Rhode Island,

Pennsylvania, and Delaware had never had any Established Church; and New York and New Jersey retained only vestiges of their former connection with the Episcopal and Dutch Reformed Churches.

When we consider the matter of religious tests, which was the only religious matter definitely dealt with at the federal Constitutional Convention, we find them as a qualification for office held over from colonial times by many of the original thirteen states. Maryland and Massachusetts required a belief "in the Christian religion." Georgia, New Hampshire, New Jersey, and North Carolina had Protestant tests. The most theological was in Delaware, where the requirement adopted in 1776 included "faith in God the Father, and in Jesus Christ, His only Son, and in the Holy Ghost, One God, blessed forever more." Some of the states had further requirements as to belief in the inspiration of the Bible, and one, Pennsylvania, demanded the belief that God was "the rewarder of the good and the punisher of the wicked."

As to the general attitude toward religion and religious freedom which prevailed in this country in its formative years, there is evidence to the effect that in spite of much indifference toward regular attendance at public worship both were held in high regard and indeed considered indispensable for the rising republic. However, the trend of developments in the church situation at the time the government was formed can be understood only as we have a clear picture of the attitude of the churches toward the colonial cause during the preceding Revolutionary period.

With the exception of the Anglicans, who had taken an oath of allegiance to the king, the major religious bodies supported the colonial cause. Among the Protestants, three groups of ministers were specially active in backing the Revolution: the Congregationalists of New England, the Presbyterians of the middle colonies, and the Baptists generally. Although the Episcopal [Anglican] clergy (including the Methodists who were still under Episcopal aegis) generally opposed it, the laity, especially in Virginia and South Carolina, included some of the most influential patriots. The Lutherans have a strong tradition of Church and State separation and have in the past been inclined to leave political matters severely alone. During the American Revolution, the Lutheran churches on the whole seem to have preserved their traditional attitude of aloofness from civil strife. There were exceptions, however, particularly among the Muhlenberg family, who ardently supported the Revolution.

Although the Roman Catholic clergy as such took little active part in promoting the patriotic cause, Catholics were sympathetic to it. There were practically no Tories* among them. This fact is the more remarkable in view of the anti-Catholic feeling which had always been latent and which had been lashed into a good deal of a fury by the Quebec Act.[6]

At the beginning of the Revolution Jews in the United States were counted by the hundreds, rather than by many thousands. Their total did not reach ten thousand until well after its close, but about one hundred men served in the American army or navy. On the whole they had been well treated in their principal settlements, Newport, Rhode Island, New York City, Philadelphia, and Charleston, South Carolina; therefore most of their leaders decided to support the colonies, realizing that the cause of American democracy and of religious freedom went hand in hand.

The New Faith in Humanity

The idea of progress, which had become so dominant toward the close of the eighteenth century, should be added to the factors contributing to the development of complete religious freedom in the United States. This idea was due largely to the Enlightenment, which assumed not only the worth and potentiality of man but his right to do his own thinking; it held out glorious future for humanity if it would only work intelligently toward its goal. In fact, as has often been pointed out, the Enlightenment really constituted a new religious faith, with human progress as its goal. A movement for the enfranchisement of the human spirit and the attainment of great new social ends for the world was in the air.

Paine's writings gave recognition to these ideas and introduced them to the public at large, as did, to a more limited group, those of Joel Barlow, especially his *Columbiad* (1807). This took the ground that human nature and human institutions had an amazing opportunity for fresh, untrammeled development in America, if the effort were only made with sufficient earnestness and intelligence. Barlow saw in his vision of democracy in the new land "the last ascending steps of the creating God."[7]

---

* The British Tory Party was based ideologically on support of the King, as against the Whigs, who wanted more power for Parliament and were more sympathetic to American complaints.

[6] Peter Guilday, *The Life and Times of John Carroll*, pp. 77 ff.

[7] Joel Barlow, *The Columbiad*, I, p. 39, as quoted in Merle Curti, *The Growth of American Thought*, p. 174.

Faith in progress was enormously stimulated by the fact that the United States was a virgin continent as far as Western civilization was concerned. Here were vast areas which none but the Indians had ever known. The mere size of the continent, its plains, mountains, lakes and rivers, forests, waterfalls, minerals, fertile lands—what we call today natural resources—all gave a sense of latent power and made the settlers feel that they had an opportunity to do creative work of a new character. This was strengthened by the inherited conviction of Puritans that New England was a New Canaan and that here they might work out their religious ideals. The citizens of the emerging United States were virtually all Christians. They differed much in matters of church membership and loyalty, in theological belief, and even, especially in the middle colonies, in national background, but they were one in their realization that God was their Father and they were His children, that there was in all of them a spark of the divine life which made them capable of great things if they would live worthy of their birthright.

And so, through a combination of the ideas of the Enlightenment and the ideals of the Christian religion, together with the fact of the unspoiled land that lay around them, and the absence of most of the hampering bonds of an old civilization, they could start out on a new experiment in community living. One of its major features would be a fair field and no special favor for any religious body, with the old causes of jealousy due to favoritism removed and with an opportunity for religious groups to dwell together in peace with much mutual sympathy and cooperation. . . .

No list of the more important factors which produced the American system of Church–State separation—one of the distinctive contributions of America to the idea of government—would be complete without some reference to the extraordinary group of statesmen in America in the last third of the eighteenth century, and especially from 1775 to 1790. These men, and a few farsighted ministers of religion who supported them, were convinced that the emerging federal government should have no connection with any Church and that religious freedom should prevail. There were a dozen or more such men whose ability and vision it would be hard to match in one country in any other time in history. Several of them, notably Jefferson, Madison, Mason, and Pinckney, knew the history of political philosophy and government in different parts of the world. They had liberal ideas of freedom of conscience and its demands based on the theory of the natural rights of men. It is no exaggeration to say that their contribution in bringing about the separation of Church and State, first in Virginia, then in the United States, with its resulting religious freedom, was epoch-making.

In contrast with the leaders of the same cause in the colonial period, the majority of the new group were not from New England; about half were from the South—five out of thirteen from the one state of Virginia. The Episcopal Church, which was not represented in the earlier group, now comes to the front with its laymen—Baptist ministers taking second place.

The new names are thirteen in number. . . . They are Benjamin Franklin, nominal Episcopalian with Presbyterian background, Deist in belief; John Witherspoon, Presbyterian; George Mason, Episcopalian; Isaac Backus, Baptist; George Washington, Episcopalian; Patrick Henry, Episcopalian, with Presbyterian affiliations; Samuel Livermore, Episcopalian; Thomas Paine, Deist; John Carroll, Roman Catholic; Thomas Jefferson, nominal Episcopalian, Deist in belief; James Madison, Episcopalian; Charles Pinckney, Episcopalian; John Leland, Baptist.

Principal Causes Which Render Religion Powerful in America (1835)*

Alexis de Tocqueville

It is odd that perhaps the most astute observer of American social and political life should have been a Frenchman, Alexis de Tocqueville. His perceptive eye and objective spirit caught American realities with a clarity that has yet to be matched, and *Democracy in America*, his book chronicling and discussing his observations, is accepted as a classic analysis. During his visit to the United States in 1831, De Tocqueville found in religion and church–state relations a striking contrast to his Continental experience.

The philosophers of the eighteenth century explained in a very simple manner the gradual decay of religious faith. Religious zeal, said they, must necessarily fail the more generally liberty is established and knowledge diffused. Unfortunately, the facts by no means accord with their theory. There are certain populations in Europe whose unbelief is only equaled by their ignorance and debasement;

* Reprinted by permission of the publisher from *Democracy in America* by Alexis de Tocqueville, translated by Phillips Bradley. Copyright, 1945 by Alfred A. Knopf, Inc.

while in America, one of the freest and most enlightened nations in
the world, the people fulfill with fervor all the outward duties of
religion.

On my arrival in the United States the religious aspect of the
country was the first thing that struck my attention; and the longer
I stayed there, the more I perceived the great political consequences
resulting from this new state of things. In France I had almost
always seen the spirit of religion and the spirit of freedom marching
in opposite directions. But in America I found they were intimately
united and that they reigned in common over the same country. My
desire to discover the causes of this phenomenon increased from day
to day. In order to satisfy it I questioned the members of all the
different sects; I sought especially the society of the clergy, who are
the depositaries of the different creeds and are especially interested
in their duration. As a member of the Roman Catholic Church, I was
more particularly brought into contact with several of its priests,
with whom I became intimately acquainted. To each of these men I
expressed my astonishment and explained my doubts. I found that
they differed upon matters of detail alone, and that they all attributed
the peaceful dominion of religion in their country mainly to the
separation of church and state. I do not hesitate to affirm that during
my stay in America I did not meet a single individual, of the clergy
or the laity, who was not of the same opinion on this point.

This led me to examine more attentively than I had hitherto done
the station which the American clergy occupy in political society.
I learned with surprise that they filled no public appointments;[1]
I did not see one of them in the administration, and they are not
even represented in the legislative assemblies. In several states[2] the
law excludes them from political life; public opinion excludes them
in all. And when I came to inquire into the prevailing spirit of the

---

[1] Unless this term is applied to the functions which many of them fill in the
schools. Almost all education is entrusted to the clergy.

[2] See the Constitution of New York, Art. VII, § 4:

"And whereas the ministers of the Gospel are, by their profession, dedicated to
the service of God and the care of souls, and ought not to be diverted from the
great duties of their functions; therefore no minister of the Gospel, or priest of
any denomination whatsoever, shall at any time hereafter, under any pretense
or description whatever, be eligible to, or capable of holding, any civil or military
office or place within this State."

See also the Constitutions of North Carolina, Art. XXXI; Virginia; South
Carolina, Art. I, § 23; Kentucky, Art. II, § 26; Tennessee, Art. VIII, § 1;
Louisiana, Art. II, § 22.

clergy, I found that most of its members seemed to retire of their own accord from the exercise of power, and that they made it the pride of their profession to abstain from politics.

I heard them inveigh against ambition and deceit, under whatever political opinions these vices might chance to lurk; but I learned from their discourses that men are not guilty in the eye of God for any opinions concerning political government which they may profess with sincerity, any more than they are for their mistakes in building a house or in driving a furrow. I perceived that these ministers of the Gospel eschewed all parties, with the anxiety attendant upon personal interest. These facts convinced me that what I had been told was true; and it then became my object to investigate their causes and to inquire how it happened that the real authority of religion was increased by a state of things which diminished its apparent force. These causes did not long escape my researches.

The short space of threescore years can never content the imagination of man; nor can the imperfect joys of this world satisfy his heart. Man alone, of all created beings, displays a natural contempt of existence, and yet a boundless desire to exist; he scorns life, but he dreads annihilation. These different feelings incessantly urge his soul to the contemplation of a future state, and religion directs his musings thither. Religion, then, is simply another form of hope, and it is no less natural to the human heart than hope itself. Men cannot abandon their religious faith without a kind of aberration of intellect and a sort of violent distortion of their true nature; they are invincibly brought back to more pious sentiments. Unbelief is an accident, and faith is the only permanent state of mankind. If we consider religious institutions merely in a human point of view, they may be said to derive an inexhaustible element of strength from man himself, since they belong to one of the constituent principles of human nature.

I am aware that at certain times religion may strengthen this influence, which originates in itself, by the artificial power of the laws and by the support of those temporal institutions that direct society. Religions intimately united with the governments of the earth have been known to exercise sovereign power founded on terror and faith; but when a religion contracts an alliance of this nature, I do not hesitate to affirm that it commits the same error as a man who should sacrifice his future to his present welfare; and in obtaining a power to which it has no claim, it risks that authority which is rightfully its own. When a religion founds its empire only upon the desire of immortality that lives in every human heart, it may aspire to universal dominion; but when it connects itself with a government, it must adopt maxims which are applicable only to certain nations. Thus, in forming an alliance with a political power, religion augments its authority over a few and forfeits the hope of reigning over all.

As long as a religion rests only upon those sentiments which are the consolation of all affliction, it may attract the affections of all mankind. But if it be mixed up with the bitter passions of the world, it may be constrained to defend allies whom its interests, and not the principle of love, have given to it; or to repel as antagonists men who are still attached to it, however opposed they may be to the powers with which it is allied. The church cannot share the temporal power of the state without being the object of a portion of that animosity which the latter excites.

The political powers which seem to be most firmly established have frequently no better guarantee for their duration than the opinions of a generation, the interests of the time, or the life of an individual. A law may modify the social condition which seems to be most fixed and determinate; and with the social condition everything else must change. The powers of society are more or less fugitive, like the years that we spend upon earth; they succeed each other with rapidity, like the fleeting cares of life; and no government has ever yet been founded upon an invariable disposition of the human heart or upon an imperishable interest.

As long as a religion is sustained by those feelings, propensities, and passions which are found to occur under the same forms at all periods of history, it may defy the efforts of time; or at least it can be destroyed only by another religion. But when religion clings to the interests of the world, it becomes almost as fragile a thing as the powers of earth. It is the only one of them all which can hope for immortality; but if it be connected with their ephemeral power, it shares their fortunes and may fall with those transient passions which alone supported them. The alliance which religion contracts with political powers must needs be onerous to itself, since it does not require their assistance to live, and by giving them its assistance it may be exposed to decay.

The danger which I have just pointed out always exists, but it is not always equally visible. In some ages governments seem to be imperishable; in others the existence of society appears to be more precarious than the life of man. Some constitutions plunge the citizens into a lethargic somnolence, and others rouse them to feverish excitement. When governments seem so strong and laws so stable, men do not perceive the dangers that may accrue from a union of church and state. When governments appear weak and laws inconstant, the danger is self-evident, but it is no longer possible to avoid it. We must therefore learn how to perceive it from afar.

In proportion as a nation assumes a democratic condition of society and as communities display democratic propensities, it becomes more and more dangerous to connect religion with political institutions; for the time is coming when authority will be bandied from hand to hand, when political theories will succeed one another, and when men, laws, and constitutions will disappear or be modified from day to day, and this not for a season only, but unceasingly. Agitation and mutability are inherent in the nature of democratic republics, just as stagnation and sleepiness are the law of absolute monarchies.

If the Americans, who change the head of the government once in four years, who elect new legislators every two years, and renew the state officers every twelve months; if the Americans, who have given up the political world to the attempts of innovators, had not placed religion beyond their reach, where could it take firm hold in the ebb and flow of human opinions? Where would be that respect which belongs to it, amid the struggles of faction? And what would become of its immortality, in the midst of universal decay? The American clergy were the first to perceive this truth and to act in conformity with it. They saw that they must renounce their religious influence if they were to strive for political power, and they chose to give up the support of the state rather than to share its vicissitudes.

In America religion is perhaps less powerful than it has been at certain periods and among certain nations; but its influence is more lasting. It restricts itself to its own resources, but of these none can deprive it; its circle is limited, but it pervades it and holds it under undisputed control.

On every side in Europe we hear voices complaining of the absence of religious faith and inquiring the means of restoring to religion some remnant of its former authority. It seems to me that we must first attentively consider what ought to be *the natural state* of men with regard to religion at the present time; and when we know what we have to hope and to fear, we may discern the end to which our efforts ought to be directed.

The two great dangers which threaten the existence of religion are schism and indifference. In ages of fervent devotion men some-times abandon their religion, but they only shake one off in order to adopt another. Their faith changes its objects, but suffers no decline. The old religion then excites enthusiastic attachment or bitter enmity in either party; some leave it with anger, others cling to it with in-creased devotedness, and although persuasions differ, irreligion is unknown. Such, however, is not the case when a religious belief is secretly undermined by doctrines which may be termed negative, since they deny the truth of one religion without affirming that of any other. Prodigious revolutions then take place in the human mind, without the apparent co-operation of the passions of man, and almost without his knowledge. Men lose the objects of their fondest hopes as if through forgetfulness. They are carried away by an imper-ceptible current, which they have not the courage to stem, but which they follow with regret, since it bears them away from a faith they love to a skepticism that plunges them into despair.

In ages which answer to this description men desert their reli-gious opinions from lukewarmness rather than from dislike; they are not rejected, but they fall away. But if the unbeliever does not admit religion to be true, he still considers it useful. Regarding religious institutions in a human point of view, he acknowledges their influence upon manners and legislation. He admits that they may serve to make men live in peace and prepare them gently for the hour of death. He regrets the faith that he has lost; and as he is deprived of a treasure of which he knows the value, he fears to take it away from those who still possess it.

On the other hand, those who continue to believe are not afraid openly to avow their faith. They look upon those who do not share their persuasion as more worthy of pity than of opposition; and they are aware that to acquire the esteem of the unbelieving, they are not obliged to follow their example. They are not hostile, then, to anyone in the world; and as they do not consider the society in which they live as an arena in which religion is bound to face its thousand deadly foes, they love their contemporaries while they condemn their weaknesses and lament their errors.

As those who do not believe conceal their incredulity, and as those who believe display their faith, public opinion pronounces itself in favor of religion: love, support, and honor are bestowed upon it, and it is only by searching the human soul that we can detect the wounds which it has received. The mass of mankind, who are never without the feeling of religion, do not perceive any-thing at variance with the established faith. The instinctive desire of a future life brings the crowd about the altar and opens the hearts of men to the precepts and consolations of religion.

But this picture is not applicable to us, for there are men among us who have ceased to believe in Christianity, without adopting any other religion; others are in the perplexities of doubt and already affect not to believe; and others, again, are afraid to avow that Christian faith which they still cherish in secret.

Amid these lukewarm partisans and ardent antagonists a small number of believers exists who are ready to brave all obstacles and to scorn all dangers in defense of their faith. They have done violence to human weakness in order to rise superior to public opinion. Excited by the effort they have made, they scarcely know where to stop; and as they know that the first use which the French made of independence was to attack religion, they look upon their contemporaries with dread, and recoil in alarm from the liberty which their fellow citizens are seeking to obtain. As unbelief appears to them to be a novelty, they comprise all that is new in one indiscriminate animosity. They are at war with their age and country, and they look upon every opinion that is put forth there as the necessary enemy of faith.

Such is not the natural state of men with regard to religion at the present day, and some extraordinary or incidental cause must be at work in France to prevent the human mind from following its natural inclination and to drive it beyond the limits at which it ought naturally to stop.

I am fully convinced that this extraordinary and incidental cause is the close connection of politics and religion. The unbelievers of Europe attack the Christians as their political opponents rather than as their religious adversaries; they hate the Christian religion as the opinion of a party much more than as an error of belief; and they reject the clergy less because they are the representatives of the Deity than because they are the allies of government.

In Europe, Christianity has been intimately united to the powers of the earth. Those powers are now in decay, and it is, as it were, buried under their ruins. The living body of religion has been bound down to the dead corpse of superannuated polity; cut but the bonds that restrain it, and it will rise once more. I do not know what could restore the Christian church of Europe to the energy of its earlier days; that power belongs to God alone; but it may be for human policy to leave to faith the full exercise of the strength which it still retains.

Chapter Three

Religion and Politics in Contemporary America

Thomas Jefferson once used the metaphor of a "wall" in referring to the separation of church and state in America. Revived later in the Everson case by Justice Black, the notion of a "wall of separation" became the basis for judicial reasoning and has continued to serve as such.

Perhaps "wall" is a semantically loaded word, as Robert Hutchins has maintained, and even as a metaphor "has done what walls usually do: it has obscured the view." Whether this wall is an impregnable philosophical fortress or a temporary picket fence, the dispute must not obscure the fact that there is a dividing line somewhere between the prerogatives and powers of religion and those of the state. That the Supreme Court has been philosophically inconsistent in religious problems is apparent; whether it should take one particular line and hold to it is a matter for debate. On religion as on all other issues, the Court redefines its position and changes its course from time to time, depending to a great degree on the social temper of the day and on the changing makeup of the Court itself. The entire American system, after all, is posited upon the expeditious resolution of conflicts arising from specific issues. Seldom do we attempt to establish moral, logical, or philosophical premises for general application to particular issues and circumstances. Philosophers aim at logic and consistency; politicians often do too, but less frequently achieve these aims.

The opening selection in this chapter, written by Will Herberg, Graduate Professor of Judaic Studies and Social Philosophy at Drew University, gives us an overview of the religious scene in contemporary America, discussing both its social bases and current trends.

The three Supreme Court cases presented next take us directly to a central and intensely disputed issue: the extent to which public education can be a vehicle for governmental support of religious institutions. The cases reveal the tortuous tightrope the Court must walk to maintain a reasonable balance between religious freedom and the support of socially worthwhile causes, and the democratic premise of secular education. In the concluding articles, several interpretations of this issue further illuminate the importance and meaning of the Court's decisions.

Three Religious Communities: Unity and Tension*

Will Herberg

The basic unity of American religion is something that goes deeper than the similarities and differences of social pattern we have been examining. The basic unity of American religion is rooted in the underlying presuppositions, values, and ideals that together constitute the American Way of Life on its "spiritual" side. It is the American Way of Life that is the shared possession of all Americans and that defines the American's convictions on those matters that count most. Just as the three great religious communities are the basic subdivisions of the American people, so are the three great "communions" (as they are often called) felt to be the recognized expressions of the "spiritual" aspect of the American Way of Life. This underlying unity not only supplies the common content of the three communions; it also sets the limits within which their conflicts and tensions may operate and beyond which they cannot go.

I

For the fundamental unity of American religion, rooted in the American Way of Life, does not preclude conflict and tension; rather, in a way, it stimulates and accentuates it. Since each of the three communities recognizes itself as fitting into a tripartite scheme, each feels itself to be a minority, even the Protestants who in actual fact constitute a large majority of the American people.

---

* From *Protestant–Catholic–Jew*, by Will Herberg. Copyright © 1955, 1960 by Will Herberg. Reprinted by permission of Doubleday & Company, Inc. The version reprinted here is from Chapter X by the same title in the Anchor Books revised edition of 1960, pp. 231–246. Most of the author's footnotes have been deleted.

In this sense, as in so many others, America is pre-eminently a land of minorities.

The communal tensions in American society are of major importance in the life of the nation. So much attention is usually focused, properly, of course, on political and economic conflicts that we are only too prone to overlook or underestimate tensions on other levels of social life, particularly the religious, since religion is generally felt to be a matter that must be kept free of "controversy." Yet the religious tensions are real and significant; they have, moreover, become considerably accentuated in recent years in connection with a number of issues that have emerged into public life, centering on the problem of church and state. Such is the peculiar structure of American religious institutionalism under the constitutional doctrine of "separation" that every tension between religious communities, however deep and complex it may actually be, tends to express itself as a conflict over church-state relations. This approach is perhaps as useful a way as any of focusing the religio-communal tensions in American life.

American Catholics still labor under the heavy weight of the bitter memory of non-acceptance in a society overwhelmingly and self-consciously Protestant. Hardly a century has passed since Catholics in America were brutally attacked by mobs, excluded from more desirable employment, and made to feel in every way that they were unwanted aliens. Despised as foreigners of low-grade stock, detested and denounced as "minions of Rome," they early developed the minority defensiveness that led them to withdraw into their own "ghetto" with a rankling sense of grievance and to divide the world into "we" and "they." This was, for a time, the case even with the Irish, who of all Catholic immigrants found their place in American society soonest. Thomas Sugrue recalls from his childhood:

> I began to hear what came to be familiar phrases: "those people," "the Prods," "our own kind," "they don't want us." I became aware that we did not live in a community of friendly neighbors, but that as Catholics we were camped instead in the middle of warlike Protestants, who didn't want us and wouldn't let us "get ahead." ... When I was twelve, a Protestant boy invited me to join the Boy Scouts ... I asked my mother, and she said no. "They don't want you," she added, "they're all Protestants." ... About this time, too, I began to hear the phrase, "They have everything." The Protestants, of course, were "they."[1]

---

[1] Thomas Sugrue, *A Catholic Speaks His Mind on America's Religious Conflict* (Evanston, Ill.: Harper and Row, 1951), pp. 47–48.

These feelings of rejection, exclusion, and grievance, though they no longer correspond to the facts of American life, and though they are deplored by more thoughtful Catholics, are still a real force among the great mass of Catholic people in this country. It takes a long time for such wounds to heal.

Partly in the interest of corporate survival in a hostile world, though basically in line with the demands and teachings of the church, Catholics in America have built up a vast and complex system of parallel institutions, the most important and pervasive of which are the church schools operating at every academic level. Though initiated under other circumstances, these parallel institutions soon fell in rather neatly with the emerging religio-communal pattern of American life. At the same time, the development of these institutions no doubt helped accentuate that tradition of Catholic "separatism" which has recently come under the criticism of Catholics themselves.

American Catholics generally seem to feel that their Catholic educational institutions, particularly the parochial schools, are much misunderstood and regarded with undue hostility by non-Catholics. They also feel themselves unjustly dealt with since they are taxed for the maintenance of "neutral" public schools they cannot in conscience use, but are denied adequate support for the Catholic schools so many of their children attend and which in actuality form part of the nation's educational system. This issue—about which no clear-cut decision is possible, since religious schools are in fact granted certain types of government assistance but are denied others—has become exacerbated in recent years and has served to bring the larger question of church–state relations into the area of bitter controversy as the focus of religio-communal conflict in present-day America.

Minority defensiveness breeds aggressiveness, intensifies separatism, and accentuates prejudice. Many Catholics still, as in earlier days, attempt to sustain their corporate self-esteem by an attitude that makes Protestant almost equivalent to unbeliever, or in more modern terminology, to "secularist." But authoritative Catholic opinion is increasingly taking another line of ideological defense—that Catholicism is, in fact, a true expression of Americanism and that the genuine Catholic position on church and state is fully in line with American tradition and experience. The extensive system of Catholic institutions is interpreted in terms of the emerging community structure of American society, involving no more separatism than any other aspect of community organization. By and large, American Catholicism has succeeded in shifting the ground of self-understanding and self-justification from the earlier negative defensiveness to a more positive affirmation of its legitimate place in the tripartite America of today. The Catholic attitude is increasingly that of a substantial minority with a strong sense of self-assurance.

Protestantism in America today presents the anomaly of a strong majority group with a growing minority consciousness. "The psychological basis of much of American Protestantism," *Social Action* (Congregational) somewhat ruefully pointed out in 1952, "lies in a negative rejection of Roman Catholicism. . . . The one emotional loyalty that of a certainty binds us [Protestants] together . . . is the battle against Rome."[2] The fear of "Rome" is indeed the most powerful cement of Protestant community consciousness, and it seems to loom larger today than it has for some time. Discussion of Protestant communal affairs moves increasingly under the shadow of the "Catholic problem," and Protestant attitudes tend more and more to be defined in terms of confrontation with a self-assured and aggressive Catholicism. The tension here has become really acute.

The fear of Catholic domination of the United States would seem to be hardly borne out by statistics. In the period from 1926 to 1950 church membership in this country increased 59.8 per cent, as against a 28.6 per cent increase in population. The Catholic Church grew 53.9 per cent, but in the same period Protestantism increased 63.7 per cent. Moreover, Protestant proselytism seemed to be more intensive and successful than Catholic. Most of the Protestant margin of increase, however, was accounted for by the expansion of the Baptists, especially the Southern Baptists. The churches affiliated with the National Council grew only 47 per cent, falling short of the total increase as well as of the comparable Roman Catholic growth.[3] In those parts of the country where Protestants and Catholics come into more direct contact, particularly in the urban centers, the Catholic Church has been making considerable headway.

But it is not this numerical growth, such as it is, that so deeply disquiets the Protestant consciousness, for, after all, the Protestant–Catholic balance has remained pretty steady in the past thirty years.

---

[2] "Christian Faith and the Protestant Churches," *Social Action*, XVIII (May, 1952), 1.

[3] See "Trends of Church Membership in the Larger Religious Bodies," *Information Service* (March 8, 1952).

Neither is it entirely the mounting intellectual prestige that American Catholicism has been acquiring from the work of a number of artists, philosophers, and writers, mostly European. What seems to be really disturbing many American Protestants is the sudden realization that Protestantism is no longer identical with America, that Protestantism has, in fact, become merely one of three communions (or communities) with equal status and equal legitimacy in the American scheme of things. This sudden realization, shocking enough when one considers the historical origins of American life and culture, appears to have driven Protestantism into an essentially defensive posture, in which it feels itself a mere minority threatened with Catholic domination.

This minority-group defensiveness has contributed greatly toward turning an important segment of American Protestantism into a vehement champion of an extreme doctrine of the separation of church and state, of religion and education, despite a disturbed awareness of the growing "religious illiteracy" of the American people. This minority-group defensiveness and fear of "Rome" have tended to drive American Protestantism into a strange alliance with the militant secularist anti-Catholicism that is associated with the recent work of Paul Blanshard. It would seem to be of some significance that the contemporary Protestant case against Catholicism is not primarily religious or theological, as it was in previous centuries, but is characteristically secular: Catholicism, we are told, is un-American, undemocratic, alien to American ways, and prone to place loyalty to church above loyalty to state and nation. Particularly shocking to many Protestants is the Catholic insistence on by-passing the public schools and educating their children in their own religious institutions. The "neutral" public school, inculcating a common national ideology above religious "divisiveness," has in fact become to large numbers of Protestants the symbol of their cause in the face of dreaded Catholic encroachment.

This argument of Catholic "divisiveness" seems to loom largest in the American Protestant mind. It has been given persuasive expression in a much-noted editorial in *The Christian Century*, entitled "Pluralism—National Menace."[4] "The threat of a plural society based on religious differences" confronts the nation, the editorial asserts, and the prime promoters of this threat are the Catholics. Pluralism, which is defined in J. S. Furnivall's formulation as a society "comprising two or more elements which live side by side,

---

[4] *The Christian Century* (June 13, 1951).

yet without mingling, in one political unit," is said to have become the deliberate and conscious policy of American Catholicism in recent years. "The proliferation of Catholic parochial schools, Catholic labor unions, Catholic civic clubs, Catholic veterans' organizations, Catholic political lobbies," the editorial concludes, "has more than religious significance to American society. It means that a conscious and well-planned large-scale attempt is being made to separate Catholics from other Americans in almost every area of social life. It means that an effort is under way to create a separate social order which will exist side by side with the rest of American society in the same political unit, but will as far as possible limit its contact with that society to the market place."

The radical evil of a plural society, we are told, is that "it can have no common will; it makes for national instability; it puts an undue emphasis on material things; [and] it nullifies the unifying function of education." The last point, which seems most basic, again raises the question of the "divisive" parochial school. "A plural society," it is alleged, "nullifies the unifying function of education by splitting up among its constituent units the responsibility for providing education, rather than allowing the state to provide a common education for all children." In a most curious way, the authoritarian doctrine of *l'état enseignant* (the "teaching state," the state as the molder of the ideology of its citizens) has become part of the creed of a large segment of American Protestantism.

Pluralism in Furnivall's sense would indeed be a serious matter for a society such as ours. But there would seem to be little danger of it in contemporary America. Indeed, *The Christian Century* appears to have discovered the menace precisely at a time when, due to advanced acculturation and increasing mobility, American Catholics are becoming increasingly integrated into the general community rather than the reverse. But this integration is taking place in a new and characteristic fashion, in and through the religious community as one of the three "pools" in the "triple melting pot" that is America. This *The Christian Century* writer apparently does not see, yet his outburst of alarm is not unrelated to the sociological process.

American Protestantism is so apprehensive at the development of religio-communal pluralism in part at least because in this kind of pluralistic situation it would seem to be at a serious disadvantage. It has been so long identified with America as a whole that it has neither the background nor the conviction necessary to build up its own Protestant community institutions in the same way that Jews

and Catholics have built up theirs. Jews and Catholics have their
own war veterans' associations, but it would probably appear strange
and unwholesome to Protestants to establish a Protestant war veterans' organization; aren't the "general" war veterans' organizations sufficiently Protestant? Once they were, just as until the last
quarter of the nineteenth century the public schools were virtually
Protestant "parochial" schools, but they are no longer such today.
Protestants, particularly the old-line Protestant leadership, cannot
seem to reconcile themselves to this primary fact. Nor do they seem
capable of overcoming, in many cases even of mitigating, the frag-
mentation of denominationalism, which places Protestantism at
another disadvantage in the face of an ecclesiastically united Catholicism. All this contributes to the Protestant distaste for "pluralism"
and adds fuel to Protestant defensive resentment against "Rome."

It would be gravely misleading, however, to leave the impression
that this attitude is universal among Protestants or that there are
no Protestant voices urging other counsels. There is, in the first
place, a striking difference in outlook between the older and the
younger generations of Protestants in America. The older generation, still thinking of America as the Protestant nation of their youth,
cannot help feeling bitter and resentful at what must appear to them
to be menacing encroachments of Catholics in American life; the
younger generation, accustomed to America as a three-religion country, cannot understand what the excitement is all about: "After all,
we're all Americans . . ." On the other side, theologically concerned
Protestants find it difficult to go along with the kind of negative
"anti-Romanism" current in many Protestant circles; they find it
both too sterile and too secularist, too reminiscent of cultural total-
ism, for their taste. Reinhold Niebuhr, John C. Bennett, Robert
McAfee Brown, Angus Dun, Liston Pope, Henry P. Van Dusen, and
other Protestant theologians, while criticizing what they regard as
erroneous views and abuses of power among Catholics, have been
particularly insistent on the necessity of a new Protestant orienta-
tion more in conformity with the facts of American life and more
faithful to its own religious tradition.

Minority consciousness is, of course, particularly strong among
American Jews, and it is among American Jews that the "philo-
ophy" and strategy of minority-group defensiveness has been most
elaborately developed. "Defense" activities play a major part in
American Jewish community life: the "defense" is against "defama-

tion" (anti-Semitism) on the one hand, and against the intrusion of
the "church" into education and public life on the other. Spokesmen
of American Jewish institutions and agencies—no one, of course, can
speak for American Jewry as a whole—have almost always displayed
an attitude on matters of church and state, religion and public affairs,
more extreme even than that of the Protestant champions of the
"wall of separation." Their alliance with secularism is even closer;
perhaps it would be more accurate to say that they have themselves
taken over the entire secularist ideology on church–state relations
to serve as defensive strategy.

It is not difficult to understand why an extreme secularism and
"separationism" should appeal to so many American Jews as a
defensive necessity. At bottom, this attitude may be traced to the
conviction, widely held though rarely articulated, that because the
Western Jew achieved emancipation with the secularization of society, he can preserve his free and equal status only so long as culture
and society remains secular. Let but religion gain a significant place
in the everyday life of the community, and the Jew, because he is
outside the bounds of the dominant religion, will once again be rele-
gated to the margins of society, displaced, disfranchised culturally
if not politically, shorn of rights and opportunities. The intrusion of
religion into education and public life, the weakening of the "wall
of separation" between religion and the state, is feared as only too
likely to result in situations in which Jews would find themselves at
a disadvantage—greater isolation, higher "visibility," an accentua-
tion of minority status. The most elementary defensive strategy
would thus seem to dictate keeping religion out of education and
public life at all costs; hence the passionate attachment of so many
American Jews to the secularist-Protestant interpretation of the
principle of "separation" and to the general "Blanshardite" position.

The defensive necessities of Jewish minority interests do not, in
the case of most Jews, seem to imply any particular tension with
Protestants, especially the more "liberal" Protestants in the big
cities where Jews are to be found; suspicion and tension emerge,
however, more obviously in Jewish–Catholic relations. A recent sur-
vey indicated that more than three times as many Jews felt themselves "interfered with" by Catholics as by Protestants, almost twice
as many Jews felt they were "looked down upon" by Catholics as by
Protestants, and three times as many Jews confessed to harboring
"ill feeling" toward Catholics as toward Protestants.[5] Catholicism

---

[5] See "What We Think of Each Other," *The Catholic Digest* (February, 1953).

represents, to many Jews, a much more aggressive form of religion
than Protestantism (most Jews never come into contact with the
militant fundamentalism of rural and small-town America) ; deep
down, it is the Catholic Church that is suspected of untoward designs
and Catholic domination that is feared.

The precarious minority position of the American Jew in a non-
Jewish world also impels him to strenuous, and what to some might
seem extravagant, efforts at corporate self-validation. The extensive
building programs that are being feverishly pursued by Jewish communities throughout the land are not merely the reflection of unparalleled prosperity and a rising level of synagogue affiliation;
these programs serve a public relations function which is never
entirely unconscious. Indeed, public relations seems to be more anx-
iously, and skillfully, cultivated by American Jewry than by either
the Catholics or the Protestants ; nothing that any Jewish community
agency does, whatever may be its intrinsic nature or value, is ever
without its public relations angle. A curious manifestation of this
concern with corporate self-validation in the face of the "outside"
world is the extraordinarily high salaries Jewish rabbis receive in
comparison with those received by Protestant ministers of equal
status and service. The salary and style of life of the rabbi is, to a
Jewish community outside the very big cities, a significant form of
vicariously defining and enhancing its corporate status in the larger
society. It is felt to be humiliating to the entire Jewish community
if the rabbi cannot maintain a manner of life that would make him
at home in the upper strata—something that would never occur to
the average Protestant community, which hardly expects its minister to achieve equal standing with the social elite. Considerations of
minority-group validation and defense thus enter into every phase
and aspect of Jewish life in America.

Religio-communal tensions have grown in recent years, particularly Protestant–Catholic tensions in most parts of the country.
Because of these tensions, which are in some sense inherent in the
situation in which we find ourselves as we undergo the transition
from a "Protestant nation" to a "three-religion country," the religious community has tended to be turned into a self-enclosed defensive institution. Catholicism maintains its communal solidarity
through a strong emphasis on a common faith and tradition, and
through a pervasive system of ecclesiastical control. The unity of

American Jewry is not the unity of religious affiliation, but rather an impalpable unity of history and destiny expressed through common institutions of philanthropy, public relations, and communal welfare; such denominationalism as exists is, therefore, without real divisive effect. American Protestantism, however, possesses neither a common tradition, nor an ecclesiastical machinery, nor an armature of community institutions. It is therefore at a grave disadvantage in the struggle for security and status that characterizes religious community life in America today.

Yet *The Christian Century* editorialist had little reason to despair, either for Protestantism or the nation. The structure of American society being what it is, no large-scale defections from Protestantism to Catholicism seem probable in the foreseeable future. The American Protestant may, on occasion, move from one denomination to another as convenience and association dictate, but under normal circumstances (barring intermarriage, and much more rarely, conversion) he will not leave the Protestant fold, for it is Protestantism that gives him his "brand name" in the bewildering complexity of American society, and "brand names" are not easily changed. American Protestantism will maintain itself and grow with the general growth of church membership and religious affiliation in this country. Whether it will prove able to recover the initiative and overcome the paralyzing negativism which burdens it today, whether it will once again become a dynamic religious movement with a new and creative word for America, only the future can tell.

Nor need we be unduly disturbed lest the growing religio-communal pluralism disrupt the unity and subvert the foundations of American society. However severe the tensions, however deep the suspicions that divide Protestant and Catholic and Jew, there are limits beyond which they cannot go. In the last analysis, Protestant and Catholic and Jew stand united through their common anchorage in, and common allegiance to, the American Way of Life. The "unifying" function of education is not annulled because Catholics have their own schools and Jews attempt to inculcate their children with a loyalty to their "people." The same basic values and ideals, the same underlying commitment to the American Way of Life, are promoted by parochial school and public school, by Catholic, Protestant, and Jew, despite the diversity of formal religious creed. After all, are not Protestantism, Catholicism, and Judaism, in their sociological actuality, alike "religions of democracy"? Are they not essentially, from this aspect at least, variant expressions of the same "common religion" which, as Williams insists, "every functioning society has to an important degree" and which supplies "an overarching sense of unity" even when that society is "riddled with conflicts"?[6] The unity of American life is a unity in multiplicity; it is a unity that is grounded in a "common faith" and is therefore capable of being re-established, despite tension and conflict, on the level of "interfaith."

II

The interfaith movement, which has assumed considerable dimensions in recent years, emerged in its present form in the early 1920's. In 1923, in order to counter the bigotry that was spreading through the nation under the growing influence of the Ku Klux Klan, the Federal Council of Churches set up a Commission on Good Will Between Jews and Christians. By 1928 it was deemed wiser to establish the movement on its own foundations, and in that year the National Conference of Christians and Jews was launched as a joint organization of "Protestants, Catholics, and Jews" with the stated purpose "to promote justice, amity, understanding, and co-operation among Protestants, Catholics, and Jews."

The activities of the N.C.C.J., largely educational in the broad sense of the term, have been conducted on the familiar tripartite basis; for example, speaking tours of teams comprising a Protestant minister, a Catholic priest, and a Jewish rabbi have been arranged, conferences on human relations have been set up, a widely syndicated news service and much pamphlet literature issued, all in line with the basic purposes of the movement. In furtherance of these purposes, moreover, a Brotherhood Week was launched in 1934 during the week of Washington's Birthday and has been observed ever since on a constantly expanding scale. The Conference has repeatedly insisted that its purpose is neither to sponsor nor to oppose "joint worship, exchange of pulpits, or common observance of holy days," but simply to "promote brotherhood in those ways which are acceptable to Protestants, Catholics, and Jews," and to serve as a "civic agency" for "affirmative co-operative action among Protestants, Catholics, and Jews in areas of common civic concern." From the beginning, "tolerance" and "co-operation" have been its most familiar watchwords.

---

[6] Robin M. Williams, *American Society: a Sociological Interpretation* (New York: Alfred A. Knopf, Inc., 1951), p. 312.

But, of course, interfaith activities in this sense have not been limited to the program of the National Conference of Christians and Jews. On a local and national scale these activities have been growing steadily in widening areas. Most college campuses have interfaith organizations or committees. Thanksgiving is increasingly observed as an interfaith holiday. New York and other cities have a special Interfaith Day with appropriate ceremonies. The struggle against Communism is organized as an interfaith venture. Conferences on alcoholism, juvenile delinquency, and other social problems are run on an interfaith basis. In fact, virtually every civic enterprise possessing any moral, cultural, or spiritual aspect is today thought of, and where possible organized, along interfaith — that is, tripartite — lines. This is, in part, frequently a matter of "political" expediency, but the interfaith pattern has extended far beyond such necessity; the very notion of tripartite arrangement is something that increasingly commends itself to the American mind as intrinsically right and proper because it is so obviously American and so obviously all-inclusive of the total American community.

This is not to say that the tensions and anxieties that divide American religious communities have not invaded the field of interfaith. Quite the contrary; the familiar themes of religio-communal suspicion reappear in this area and are on occasion given overt expression. Thus, Catholics are constantly concerned that interfaith should not lead to "interreligious worship" or "interreligious theological discussion" or to the notion that "one religion is as good as another." Protestants and Jews seem perpetually disturbed lest interfaith be subverted by Catholics into an instrument of corporate aggrandizement. But on the whole, each recognizes a need and a responsibility that overrides, if it does not dispel, all suspicions and doubts. The interfaith movement has emerged as one of the most vigorous and extensive enterprises on the American scene; above all, the interfaith idea has become one of the accepted aspects of the American Way of Life.

It is hardly accidental that the interfaith enterprise, which flourishes so vigorously in the United States, has never been able to make much headway in Britain, on the European continent, or elsewhere in the world. Similar organizations have been set up in various countries, beginning with a conference in London in November, 1924, but these have led a rather tenuous existence, with a very limited scope of activities; much the same can be said of the world organization launched at an international conference held in Oxford in August, 1946. Most of these ventures outside the United States have either been emergency agencies to fight anti-Semitism, and have generally lapsed with the waning of the danger, or they have been converted into vehicles of theological discussion. It is this latter enterprise—the so-called "Jewish–Christian conversation"—that is characteristic of the "interfaith" idea on the continent, rather than the religio-communal co-operation familiar in this country.

The contrast is striking and significant. The American kind of interfaith, operative at all levels of civic life, but carefully steering clear of religious or theological discussion, makes little appeal to the European to whom the tripartite system is strange and who feels that religiously concerned people should be interested in mutual discussion of their theological positions. In this country, on the other hand, controversial discussion of religion in which each participant confesses and bears witness to his convictions is felt to be undesirable and "un-American," since it might tend to accentuate "ideological" differences rather than stress commitment to the shared values and ideals of the American Way of Life. One's particular religion is, of course, to be cherished and loyally adhered to, but it is not felt to be something that one "flaunts" in the face of people of other faiths. When at the Second Assembly of the World Council of Churches at Evanston, in August, 1954, the proposal was made to include a special reference to Christian evangelical witness to the Jews in the message to the churches, Charles P. Taft, lay delegate of the Protestant Episcopal Church of the United States, "objected strongly to the reference. Insisting that his views had no political implications, he said that the reference would make for bad interfaith relations . . ."[7] The special reference to the Jews was deleted by a vote of 195 to 150. In Europe, an omission of such reference to the Jews would very likely have been regarded as an outcropping of anti-Semitic prejudice, reminiscent of the Nazi exclusion of the Jews from the scope of the church; in the United States, to include such reference was felt by even earnest Christians to be somehow insulting to the Jews and an impairment of interfaith relations! It will be noted how big this American idea of "interfaith relations" is beginning to loom in church councils even on the highest level.

---

[7] "Literalists Lose by Close Vote," *The Christian Century* (September 8, 1954).

Interfaith in this country is the device that American experience has elaborated for bringing some measure of harmony among the religious communities and in some degree mitigating their tensions and suspicions. It is made possible by their common grounding in the American Way of Life and their feeling that despite all differences of creed, "brotherhood" and "affirmative co-operative action" among Protestants, Catholics, and Jews is not only possible and desirable but is also in a sense mandatory if American democracy is to function properly. Interfaith in the American sense is America's answer to the problem of religious divisiveness in a society structured along religio-communal lines.

Everson v. Board of Education (1947)*

The Everson case, like the following two Supreme Court decisions, is noteworthy as an attempt to deal with the problem of "separation" in a legal rather than a philosophical manner. The specific question presented was whether state legislation (in New Jersey here) could continue to provide for the reimbursement of public transportation costs to the parents of children attending parochial schools. The case found its way to the Supreme Court on appeal by the plaintiff, Everson, who maintained that public monies were, in essence, being used to support an establishment of religion and that the New Jersey statute thereby violated the First and Fourteenth Amendments to the United States Constitution. The Supreme Court, holding against Everson, sought to clarify "separation" by finding "that the [First] Amendment requires the state to be a neutral in its relations with groups of religious believers and non-believers; it does not require the state to be their adversary." The decision was written by Justice Black.

The New Jersey statute is challenged as a "law respecting an establishment of religion." The First Amendment, as made applicable to the states by the Fourteenth, *Murdock* v. *Pennsylvania*, 319 U.S. 105, commands that a state "shall make no law respecting an establishment of religion, or prohibiting the free exercise thereof. . . ." Whether this New Jersey law is one respecting an "establishment of religion" requires an understanding of the meaning of that language, particularly with respect to the imposition of taxes. Once again, therefore, it is not inappropriate briefly to review the background and environment of the period in which that constitutional language was fashioned and adopted.

---

* 330 U.S. 1, 91 L.Ed. 711, 168 A.L.R. 1392, 67 S.Ct. 504.

A large proportion of the early settlers of this country came here from Europe to escape the bondage of laws which compelled them to support and attend government-favored churches. The centuries immediately before and contemporaneous with the colonization of America had been filled with turmoil, civil strife, and persecutions, generated in large part by established sects determined to maintain their absolute political and religious supremacy. With the power of government supporting them, at various times and places, Catholics had persecuted Protestants, Protestants had persecuted Catholics, Protestant sects had persecuted other Protestant sects, Catholics of one shade of belief had persecuted Catholics of another shade of belief, and all of these had from time to time persecuted Jews. In efforts to force loyalty to whatever religious group happened to be on top and in league with the government of a particular time and place, men and women had been fined, cast in jail, cruelly tortured, and killed. Among the offenses for which these punishments had been inflicted were such things as speaking disrespectfully of the views of ministers of government-established churches, non-attendance at those churches, expressions of non-belief in their doctrines, and failure to pay taxes and tithes to support them.

These practices of the Old World were transplanted to and began to thrive in the soil of the new America. The very charters granted by the English Crown to the individuals and companies designated to make the laws which would control the destinies of the colonials authorized these individuals and companies to erect religious establishments which all, whether believers or non-believers, would be required to support and attend. An exercise of this authority was accompanied by a repetition of many of the Old World practices and persecutions. Catholics found themselves hounded and proscribed because of their faith; Quakers who followed their conscience went to jail; Baptists were peculiarly obnoxious to certain dominant Protestant sects; men and women of varied faiths who happened to be in a minority in a particular locality were persecuted because they steadfastly persisted in worshipping God only as their own consciences dictated. And all of these dissenters were compelled to pay tithes and taxes to support government-sponsored churches whose ministers preached inflammatory sermons designed to strengthen and consolidate the established faith by generating a burning hatred against dissenters.

These practices became so commonplace as to shock the freedom-loving colonials into a feeling of abhorrence. The imposition of taxes to pay ministers' salaries and to build and maintain churches and church property aroused their indignation. It was these feelings which found expression in the First Amendment. No one locality and no one group throughout the colonies can rightly be given entire credit for having aroused the sentiment that culminated in adoption of the Bill of Rights' provisions embracing religious liberty. But Virginia, where the established church had achieved a dominant influence in political affairs and where many excesses attracted wide public attention, provided a great stimulus and able leadership for the movement. The people there, as elsewhere, reached the conviction that individual religious liberty could be achieved best under a government which was stripped of all power to tax, to support, or otherwise to assist any or all religions, or to interfere with the beliefs of any religious individual or group. . . .

The meaning and scope of the First Amendment, preventing establishment of religion or prohibiting the free exercise thereof, in the light of its history and the evils it was designed forever to suppress, have been several times elaborated by the decisions of this Court prior to the application of the First Amendment to the states by the Fourteenth. The broad meaning given the Amendment by these earlier cases has been accepted by this Court in its decisions concerning an individual's religious freedom rendered since the Fourteenth Amendment was interpreted to make the prohibitions of the First applicable to state action abridging religious freedom. There is every reason to give the same application and broad interpretation to the "establishment of religion" clause. . . .

The "establishment of religion" clause of the First Amendment means at least this: Neither a state nor the federal government can set up a church. Neither can pass laws which aid one religion, aid all religions, or prefer one religion to another. Neither can force nor influence a person to go to or to remain away from church against his will or force him to profess a belief or disbelief in any religion. No person can be punished for entertaining or professing religious beliefs or disbeliefs, for church attendance or non-attendance. No tax in any amount, large or small, can be levied to support any religious activities or institutions, whatever they may be called, or whatever form they may adopt to teach or practice religion. Neither a state nor the federal government can, openly or secretly, participate in the affairs of any religious organizations or groups and *vice versa*. In the words of Jefferson, the clause against establishment of religion by law was intended to erect "a wall of separation between church and state." *Reynolds* v. *United States, supra* at 164 [of 98 U.S.].

We must consider the New Jersey statute in accordance with the foregoing limitations imposed by the First Amendment. But we must not strike that state statute down if it is within the state's constitutional power even though it approaches the verge of that power. See *Interstate Ry.* v. *Massachusetts,* Holmes J., *supra* at 85, 88. New Jersey cannot consistently with the "establishment of religion" clause of the First Amendment contribute tax-raised funds to the support of an institution which teaches the tenets and faith of any church. On the other hand, other language of the amendment commands that New Jersey cannot hamper its citizens in the free exercise of their own religion. Consequently, it cannot exclude individual Catholics, Lutherans, Mohammedans, Baptists, Jews, Methodists, non-believers, Presbyterians, or the members of any other faith, *because of their faith, or lack of it,* from receiving the benefits of public welfare legislation. While we do not mean to intimate that a state could not provide transportation only to children attending public schools, we must be careful, in protecting the citizens of New Jersey against state-established churches, to be sure that we do not inadvertently prohibit New Jersey from extending its general state law benefits to all its citizens without regard to their religious belief.

Measured by these standards, we cannot say that the First Amendment prohibits New Jersey from spending tax-raised funds to pay the bus fares of parochial school pupils as a part of a general program under which it pays the fares of pupils attending public and other schools. It is undoubtedly true that children are helped to get to church schools. There is even a possibility that some of the children might not be sent to the church schools if the parents were compelled to pay their children's bus fares out of their own pockets when transportation to a public school would have been paid for by the state. The same possibility exists where the state requires a local transit company to provide reduced fares to school children including those attending parochial schools, or where a municipally owned transportation system undertakes to carry all school children free of charge. Moreover, state-paid policemen, detailed to protect children going to and from church schools from the very real hazards of traffic, would serve much the same purpose and accomplish much the same result as state provisions intended to guarantee free transportation of a kind which the state deems to be best for the school children's welfare. And parents might refuse to risk their children to the serious danger of traffic accidents going to and from parochial schools, the approaches to which were not protected by policemen. Similarly, parents might be reluctant to permit their children to attend schools which the state had cut off from such general government services as ordinary police and fire protection, connections for sewage disposal, public highways and sidewalks. Of course, cutting off church schools from these services, so separate and so indisputably marked off from the religious function, would make it far more difficult for the schools to operate. But such is obviously not the purpose of the First Amendment. That Amendment requires the state to be a neutral in its relations with groups of religious believers and non-believers; it does not require the state to be their adversary. State power is no more to be used so as to handicap religions than it is to favor them.

This Court has said that parents may, in the discharge of their duty under state compulsory education laws, send their children to a religious rather than a public school if the school meets the secular educational requirements which the state has power to impose. See *Pierce* v. *Society of Sisters*, 268 U.S. 510. It appears that these parochial schools meet New Jersey's requirements. The state contributes no money to the schools. It does not support them. Its legislation, as applied, does no more than provide a general program to help parents get their children, regardless of their religion, safely and expeditiously to and from accredited schools.

The First Amendment has erected a wall between church and state. That wall must be kept high and impregnable. We could not approve the slightest breach. New Jersey has not breached it here.

McCollum v. Board of Education (1948)*

A year after its Everson decision, the Supreme Court was faced once again with having to define the relationship of religion to public education, this time in regard to "released-time" religious instructions. In the McCollum case, the constitutionality of allowing religious groups to use public school facilities for voluntary religious instruction was challenged. The Court's support of the challenge and invalidation of the practice of in-school religious education puzzled many who sensed an inconsistency with the Everson decision; the Court's rationale seemed remote from the Everson dictum of "neutrality." The new decision, written again by Justice Black, stated that "the First Amendment rests upon the premise that both religion and government can best work to

---

* 333 U.S. 203, 92 L.Ed. 648, 2 A.L.R.2d 1338, 68 S.Ct. 461.

achieve their lofty aims if each is left free from the other within its respective sphere."

This case relates to the power of a state to utilize its tax-supported public school system in aid of religious instruction insofar as that power may be restricted by the First and Fourteenth Amendments to the federal Constitution.

The appellant, Vashti McCollum, began this action for mandamus against the Champaign Board of Education in the Circuit Court of Champaign County, Illinois. Her asserted interest was that of a resident and taxpayer of Champaign and of a parent whose child was then enrolled in the Champaign public schools. Illinois has a compulsory education law which, with exceptions, requires parents to send their children, aged seven to sixteen, to its tax-supported public schools where the children are to remain in attendance during the hours when the schools are regularly in session. Parents who violate this law commit a misdemeanor punishable by fine unless the children attend private or parochial schools which meet educational standards fixed by the state. District boards of education are given general supervisory powers over the use of the public school buildings within the school districts. Ill.Rev.Stat. ch. 122, §§ 123, 301 (1943).

Appellant's petition for mandamus alleged that religious teachers, employed by private religious groups, were permitted to come weekly into the school buildings during the regular hours set apart for secular teaching, and then and there for a period of thirty minutes substitute their religious teaching for the secular education provided under the compulsory education law. The petitioner charged that this joint public-school religious-group program violated the First and Fourteenth Amendments to the United States Constitution. The prayer of her petition was that the Board of Education be ordered to "adopt and enforce rules and regulations prohibiting all instruction in and teaching of religious education in all public schools in Champaign School District Number 71, . . . and in all public school houses and buildings in said district when occupied by public schools."

. . . .

Although there are disputes between the parties as to various inferences that may or may not properly be drawn from the evidence concerning the religious program, the following facts are shown by the record without dispute. In 1940 interested members of the Jewish, Roman Catholic, and a few of the Protestant faiths formed a voluntary association called the Champaign Council on Religious Education. They obtained permission from the Board of

Education to offer classes in religious instruction to public school pupils in grades four to nine inclusive. Classes were made up of pupils whose parents signed printed cards requesting that their children be permitted to attend; they were held weekly, thirty minutes for the lower grades, forty-five minutes for the higher. The council employed the religious teachers at no expense to the school authorities, but the instructors were subject to the approval and supervision of the superintendent of schools. The classes were taught in three separate religious groups by Protestant teachers, Catholic priests, and a Jewish rabbi, although for the past several years there have apparently been no classes instructed in the Jewish religion. Classes were conducted in the regular classrooms of the school building. Students who did not choose to take the religious instruction were not released from public school duties; they were required to leave their classrooms and go to some other place in the school building for pursuit of their secular studies. On the other hand, students who were released from secular study for the religious instructions were required to be present at the religious classes. Reports of their presence or absence were to be made to their secular teachers.

The foregoing facts, without reference to others that appear in the record, show the use of tax-supported property for religious instruction and the close cooperation between the school authorities and the religious council in promoting religious education. The operation of the state's compulsory education system thus assists and is integrated with the program of religious instruction carried on by separate religious sects. Pupils compelled by law to go to school for secular education are released in part from their legal duty upon the condition that they attend the religious classes. This is beyond all question a utilization of the tax-established and tax-supported public school system to aid religious groups to spread their faith. And it falls squarely under the ban of the First Amendment (made applicable to the states by the Fourteenth) as we interpreted it in *Everson* v. *Board of Education*, 330 U.S. 1. . . . The majority in the Everson case, and the minority as shown by quotations from the dissenting views in our notes 6 and 7 agreed that the First Amendment's language properly interpreted, had erected a wall of separation between church and state. They disagreed as to the facts shown by the record and as to the proper application of the First Amendment's language to those facts.

Recognizing that the Illinois program is barred by the First and Fourteenth Amendments if we adhere to the views expressed both by the majority and the minority in the Everson case, counsel for the respondents challenge those views as dicta and urge that we reconsider and repudiate them. They argue that historically the First Amendment was intended to forbid only government preference of one religion over another, not an impartial governmental assistance of all religions. In addition they ask that we distinguish or overrule our holding in the Everson case that the Fourteenth Amendment made the "establishment of religion" clause of the First Amendment applicable as a prohibition against the states. After giving full consideration to the arguments presented we are unable to accept either of these contentions.

To hold that a state cannot consistently with the First and Fourteenth Amendments utilize its public school system to aid any or all religious faiths or sects in the dissemination of their doctrines and ideals does not, as counsel urge, manifest a governmental hostility to religion or religious teachings. A manifestation of such hostility would be at war with our national tradition as embodied in the First Amendment's guaranty of the free exercise of religion. For the First Amendment rests upon the premise that both religion and government can best work to achieve their lofty aims if each is left free from the other within its respective sphere. Or, as we said in the Everson case, the First Amendment has erected a wall between Church and State which must be kept high and impregnable.

Here not only are the state's tax-supported public school buildings used for the dissemination of religious doctrines. The state also affords sectarian groups an invaluable aid in that it helps to provide pupils for their religious classes through use of the state's compulsory public school machinery. This is not separation of church and state.

The cause is reversed and remanded to the state Supreme Court for proceedings not inconsistent with this opinion.

. . . .

MR. JUSTICE JACKSON, concurring. . . . While we may and should end such formal and explicit instruction as the Champaign plan and can at all times prohibit teaching of creed and catechism and ceremonial and can forbid forthright proselyting in the schools, I think it remains to be demonstrated whether it is possible, even if desirable, to comply with such demands as plaintiff's completely to isolate and cast out of secular education all that some people may reasonably regard as religious instruction. Perhaps subjects such as mathematics, physics or chemistry are, or can be, completely secularized.

But it would not seem practical to teach either practice or appreciation of the arts if we are to forbid exposure of youth to any religious influences. Music without sacred music, architecture minus the cathedral, or painting without the scriptural themes would be eccentric and incomplete, even from a secular point of view. Yet the inspirational appeal of religion in these guises is often stronger than in forthright sermon. Even such a "science" as biology raises the issue between evolution and creation as an explanation of our presence on this planet. Certainly a course in English literature that omitted the Bible and other powerful uses of our mother tongue for religious ends would be pretty barren. And I should suppose it is a proper, if not an indispensable, part of preparation for a worldly life to know the roles that religion and religions have played in the tragic story of mankind. The fact is that, for good or for ill, nearly everything in our culture worth transmitting, everything which gives meaning to life, is saturated with religious influences, derived from paganism, Judaism, Christianity—both Catholic and Protestant—and other faiths accepted by a large part of the world's peoples. One can hardly respect a system of education that would leave the student wholly ignorant of the currents of religious thought that move the world society for a part in which he is being prepared. . . .

The task of separating the secular from the religious in education is one of magnitude, intricacy and delicacy. To lay down a sweeping constitutional doctrine as demanded by complainant and apparently approved by the Court, applicable alike to all school boards of the nation, "to immediately adopt and enforce rules and regulations prohibiting all instruction in and teaching of religious education in all public schools," is to decree a uniform, rigid and, if we are consistent, an unchanging standard for countless school boards representing and serving highly localized groups which not only differ from each other but which themselves from time to time change attitudes. It seems to me that to do so is to allow zeal for our own ideas of what is good in public instruction to induce us to accept the role of a super board of education for every school district in the nation. . . .

MR. JUSTICE REED, dissenting. . . .

It seems clear to me that the "aid" referred to by the Court in the Everson case could not have been those incidental advantages that religious bodies, with other groups similarly situated, obtain as a byproduct of organized society. This explains the well-known fact that all churches receive "aid" from government in the form of freedom from taxation. The Everson decision itself justified the transportation of children to church schools by New Jersey for safety reasons. It accords with *Cochran* v. *Louisiana State Board of Education,* 281 U.S. 370, where this Court upheld a free textbook statute of Louisiana against a charge that it aided private schools on the ground that the books were for the education of the children, not to aid religious schools. Likewise the National School Lunch Act aids all school children attending tax-exempt schools. In *Bradfield* v. *Roberts,* 175 U.S. 291, this Court held proper the payment of money by the federal government to build an addition to a hospital, chartered by individuals who were members of a Roman Catholic sisterhood, and operated under the auspices of the Roman Catholic Church. This was done over the objection that it aided the establishment of religion. . . .

The practices of the federal government offer many examples of this kind of "aid" by the state to religion. The Congress of the United States has a chaplain for each House who daily invokes divine blessings and guidance for the proceedings. The armed forces have commissioned chaplains from early days. They conduct the public services in accordance with the liturgical requirements of their respective faiths, ashore and afloat, employing for the purpose property belonging to the United States and dedicated to the services of religion. Under the Servicemen's Readjustment Act of 1944, eligible veterans may receive training at government expense for the ministry in denominational schools. The schools of the District of Columbia have opening exercises which "include a reading from the Bible without note or comment, and the Lord's Prayer.

In the United States Naval Academy and the United States Military Academy, schools wholly supported and completely controlled by the federal government, there are a number of religious activities. Chaplains are attached to both schools. Attendance at church services on Sunday is compulsory at both the Military and Naval Academies. At West Point the Protestant services are held in the Cadet Chapel, the Catholic in the Catholic Chapel, and the Jewish in the Old Cadet Chapel; at Annapolis only Protestant services are held on the reservation, midshipmen of other religious persuasions attend the churches of the city of Annapolis. These facts indicate that both schools since their earliest beginnings have maintained and enforced a pattern of participation in formal worship. . . .

Zorach v. Clauson (1952)*

In the Zorach case, the Supreme Court was confronted by a new twist to released-time religious nstruction. Although public school machinery was used in New York City for providing and processing parental consent forms for released time, the actual religious instruction was carried on off-campus. This change of location from public to private facilities apparently carried weight sufficient to sway the Court from its stand in the McCollum case. The gist of its reasoning, presented by Justice Douglas, was that while the government may not thrust a religious doctrine upon anyone, it may suspend its operations to allow the pursuit of religious instruction by those who desire it.

This "released-time" program involves neither religious instruction in public school classrooms nor the expenditure of public funds. All costs, including the application blanks, are paid by the religious organizations. The case is therefore unlike *McCollum* v. *Board of Education*, 333 U.S. 203, which involved a released-time program from Illinois. In that case the classrooms were turned over to religious instructors. We accordingly held that the program violated the First Amendment which (by reason of the Fourteenth Amendment) prohibits the states from establishing religion or prohibiting its free exercise.

Appellants, who are taxpayers and residents of New York City and whose children attend its public schools, challenge the present law, contending it is in essence not different from the one involved in the McCollum case. Their argument, stated elaborately in various ways, reduces itself to this: the weight and influence of the school is put behind a program for religious instruction; public school teachers police it, keeping tab on students who are released; the classroom activities come to a halt while the students who are released for religious instruction are on leave; the school is a crutch on which the churches are leaning for support in their religious training; without the cooperation of the schools this released-time program, like the one in the McCollum case, would be futile and ineffective. The New York Court of Appeals sustained the law against this claim of unconstitutionality. 303 N.Y. 161, 100 N.E.2d 463. The case is here on appeal. 28 U.S.C. § 1257(2).

. . . .

It takes obtuse reasoning to inject any issue of the "free exercise" of religion into the present case. No one is forced to go to the religious classroom and no religious exercise or instruction is brought to the classrooms of the public schools. A student need not take religious

* 343 U.S. 306, 96 L.Ed. 954, 72 S.Ct. 679.

instruction. He is left to his own desires as to the manner or time of his religious devotions, if any.

There is a suggestion that the system involves the use of coercion to get public school students into religious classrooms. There is no evidence in the record before us that supports that conclusion. The present record indeed tells us that the school authorities are neutral in this regard and do no more than release students whose parents so request. If in fact coercion were used, if it were established that any one or more teachers were using their office to persuade or force students to take the religious instruction, a wholly different case would be presented. Hence we put aside that claim of coercion both as respects the "free exercise" of religion and "an establishment of religion" within the meaning of the First Amendment.

Moreover, apart from that claim of coercion, we do not see how New York by this type of released-time program has made a law respecting an establishment of religion within the meaning of the First Amendment. There is much talk of the separation of church and state in the history of the Bill of Rights and in the decisions clustering around the First Amendment. See *Everson* v. *Board of Education,* 330 U.S. 1; *McCollum* v. *Board of Education, supra.* There cannot be the slightest doubt that the First Amendment reflects the philosophy that church and state should be separated. And so far as interference with the "free exercise" of religion and an "establishment" of religion are concerned, the separation must be complete and unequivocal. The First Amendment within the scope of its coverage permits no exception; the prohibition is absolute. The First Amendment, however, does not say that in every and all respects there shall be a separation of church and state. Rather, it studiously defines the manner, the specific ways, in which there shall be no concert or union or dependency one on the other. That is the common sense of the matter. Otherwise the state and religion would be aliens to each other—hostile, suspicious, and even unfriendly.

. . . .

. . . The nullification of this law would have wide and profound effects. A Catholic student applies to his teacher for permission to leave the school during hours on a Holy Day of Obligation to attend a mass. A Jewish student asks his teacher for permission to be excused for Yom Kippur. A Protestant wants the afternoon off for a family baptismal ceremony. In each case the teacher requires parental consent in writing. In each case the teacher, in order to make sure the student is not a truant, goes further and requires a report from the priest, the rabbi, or the minister. The teacher in other words cooperates in a religious program to the extent of making it possible for her students to participate in it. Whether she does it occasionally for a few students, regularly for one, or pursuant to a systematized program designed to further the religious needs of all the students does not alter the character of the act.

We are a religious people whose institutions presuppose a Supreme Being. We guarantee the freedom to worship as one chooses. We make room for as wide a variety of beliefs and creeds as the spiritual needs of man deem necessary. We sponsor an attitude on the part of government that shows no partiality to any one group and that lets each flourish according to the zeal of its adherents and the appeal of its dogma. When the state encourages religious instruction or cooperates with religious authorities by adjusting the schedule of public events to sectarian needs, it follows the best of our traditions. For it then respects the religious nature of our people and accommodates the public service to their spiritual needs.

. . . .

. . . We follow the McCollum case. But we cannot expand it to cover the present released-time program unless separation of church and state means that public institutions can make no adjustments of their schedules to accommodate the religious needs of the people. We cannot read into the Bill of Rights such a philosophy of hostility to religion.

MR. JUSTICE BLACK, dissenting. . . .

I see no significant difference between the invalid Illinois system and that of New York here sustained. Except for the use of the school buildings in Illinois, there is no difference between the systems which I consider even worthy of mention. In the New York program, as in that of Illinois, the school authorities release some of the children on the condition that they attend the religious classes, get reports on whether they attend, and hold the other children in the school building until the religious hour is over. As we attempted to make categorically clear, the McCollum decision would have been the same if the religious classes had not been held in the school buildings. McCollum thus held that Illinois could not constitutionally manipulate the compelled classroom hours of its compulsory school machinery so as to channel children into sectarian classes. Yet that is exactly what the Court holds New York can do . . .

God, Man and the Supreme Court*

Paul Blanshard

Separation — The Zone of Agreement

All things considered, the Supreme Court has had a relatively easy time in interpreting the free-exercise-of-religion clause of the First Amendment. The overwhelming majority of Americans believe in religious freedom, and no large pressure group ventures to oppose the concept directly.

It is quite a different matter with the establishment-of-religion clause. Powerful pressure groups are constantly trying to stretch the Court's interpretation of this term to their own advantage, and some of these groups include important churches. The clause has as many legal meanings as the rainbow has variations in color, and each group of special-interest interpreters is ready to fight for its own interpretation, always under the color of religious freedom.

In this area of establishment—and its converse, separation—the zone of agreement is more traditional than logical. Many of our existing practices do not fit in with any consistent legal pattern; some are still recognized as valid only because the Supreme Court has not caught up with them.

Everybody agrees that there should be no single established church, no official national faith and no formal preference for any particular church. Even the Roman Catholic Church—which, as a world-wide power, stands for partial church establishment—does not assert its claims for such status in the United States. But in practice, at the local level, in spite of the Constitution, the non-establishment principle is fractured quite frequently in the public schools by both Catholics and Protestants. In this area, Jews as well as unbelievers have much to complain of.

Some of the establishment practices are accepted by the Court and by the people largely because they were inherited from England in colonial days. Tax exemption of church property, for example, is one of the secure traditions. It was adopted almost automatically by the new states after the Revolution, although Madison opposed the idea. So, later, did Grant, who even suggested in a message

---

* From Chapter III, "God, Man and the Supreme Court" in Paul Blanshard, *God and Man in Washington* (Boston: Beacon Press, 1960), pp. 74–84. Only documenting footnotes retained. Reprinted by permission of the Beacon Press, © 1960 by Paul Blanshard.

to Congress that only graveyards and "possibly" church buildings should be allowed religious exemptions. Congress did not adopt his suggestion.

Today there is local exemption in every state for both churches and church schools, and in most states for rectories and parsonages. Thirty-two states have some reference to tax exemption for religious organizations in their constitutions, and fifteen of them make such exemption mandatory. The Supreme Court set federal limits to this practice in 1885 by deciding that a Catholic church in Washington could not secure exemption on surrounding land "not reasonably needed" for church operation. California was the last state to exempt all religious schools; its 1952 referendum was confirmed by the Supreme Court in 1956.[1]

Is this tax exemption of religious property an illegal subsidy or merely a legitimate extension of government charity? It can be looked at either way. Certainly the Court's reasons for defending the validity of tax exemption are extremely thin, especially in the light of its strong pronouncements in the Everson and McCollum cases and its statement in the Zorach released-time case that "Government may not finance religion. . . ." But Leo Pfeffer, author of the scholarly study *Church, State, and Freedom*, is probably right in suggesting that, if a taxpayer tried to challenge the ancient policy today, the Court might not even allow him to enter its door. In fact, the Court slammed the door shut in 1956 against a challenge of California's 1952 referendum.

Sometimes special privilege acquires sanction by the mere passage of time, and the courts apply to the privilege that judicial stop sign called *stare decisis* (to stand by former decisions). It is also argued that the non-religious, social service aspects of church activity have an independent claim to exemption. Many welfare and educational enterprises are mingled with religion under the tax umbrella of the word "church," and their welfare aspects cannot be unscrambled from their purely religious aspects.

The real threat to church–state separation involved in the tax exemption of churches is didactic. Tax exemption is almost always used as the first precedent in a chain of reasoning by those who argue that the Constitution permits public money to be used for sectarian schools. The argument almost always ends with the "clincher": "Since you acknowledge that tax exemption of churches is constitutional, it must also be constitutional to subsidize sectarian schools."

---

[1] *Lundberg* v. *Alameda County*, 286 Pac. 2d 1; appeal dismissed, 352 U.S. 921.

As we shall see later, there are many missing links in this chain of logic.

Meanwhile churches and clergymen continue to receive a great many special privileges in addition to property tax exemption under both federal and state laws, and the Supreme Court does not forbid the concessions as an illegal establishment of religion under the First Amendment. Donors to churches, under Section 170 of the Internal Revenue Code, may deduct such contributions in their federal income-tax returns up to 30 per cent of net income. Most states exempt gifts to religious organizations from inheritance taxes; it has been estimated that the exemption applies to $200 million in bequests in a decade. Clergymen can buy tickets on most railroads for one-half of the first-class fare (and so one-half of the federal tax) ; the general taxpayers and stockholders pay more than their shares to make up the difference. A similar but more restricted concession to clergical air passengers was made in a 1956 amendment to the Civil Aeronautics Act.

Clergymen have been exempted from military service by federal law during both world wars, and the Court has repeatedly sustained the exemption as a constitutional choice within the power of Congress. The Court has unanimously brushed aside the argument that military exemption for clergymen is an illegal establishment of religion, simply contending that "its unsoundness is too apparent to require us to do more."[2] The Court has repeatedly confirmed the exemption of religious conscientious objectors, not as a constitutional right but as a privilege to be conferred by Congress within its general legislative powers.[3] We have already seen the well-established practice of using government funds for the salaries of chaplains in the armed forces, in prisons and in Congress itself.

All of these somewhat questionable borderline practices of semi-establishment for religion are considered within the zone of agreement between church and state largely because they have endured so long without successful challenge. The reasoning behind them partakes more of sentiment than logic. And who shall say that a Supreme Court must be immune to sentiment, especially when it has the sanction of tradition?

Separation — The Zones of Conflict

There are two great zones of disagreement about the meaning of the phrase "establishment of religion" in the First Amendment.

---

[2] 245 U.S. 366 (1918).

[3] See, for example, *United States* v. *Macintosh,* 283 U.S. 605 (1931).

One concerns public money spent for sectarian causes; the other concerns the use of public institutions for the promotion of religious ideas. The two zones overlap constantly, of course, and the issues in both are closely bound up with the problems of the free exercise of religion. Still, there are really two issues involved, not one.

The money frontier between church and state is now the line where the heaviest sectarian cannonading is in progress. The justices of the Supreme Court have had great difficulty in building between churches and the public treasury a wall that is satisfactory both to themselves and to any large segment of our population. In general, Jews, most Protestants and the unchurched want a high wall to be erected; most Catholics and some Protestants prefer a low wall that can be easily vaulted.

The key decisions in this field have concerned the use of local public funds for Catholic parochial schools. This issue did not reach the Supreme Court until 1947, partly because the Court waited until the twentieth century to interpret all the protections of the non-establishment clause of the Fourteenth Amendment as applying even on the local level. There is an analogy here between the Court's delayed action on racial segregation and its delayed action on church and state. In both cases, the Constitution has remained unchanged, but the Court has made a new law by new and up-to-date interpretations of old phrases.

May public money be constitutionally used for sectarian schools under the establishment clause? The Court's answer, embodied in three famous decisions of the 1940's, is a definite *No* for all direct appropriations for the central expenditures of such schools. No federal or local tax funds may be used for building costs, teachers' salaries or other regular operational expenses. This principle was established in the famous Everson, New Jersey, bus case in 1947, which is probably the most important case in the whole history of American church–state law. The financial reasoning was confirmed by the Court in the McCollum case in 1948 and the Zorach case in 1952.

In the Everson case, a New Jersey town, acting under a state statute, has allowed local tax funds to be used to reimburse Catholic parents for the cost of buses bringing children to parochial schools. A local taxpayer challenged this use of public money as an unconstitutional establishment of religion. The Court took a deep breath and expressed in one vital paragraph those general principles about the money frontier which now constitute American policy on the subject. On these principles the justices were unanimous. The paragraph actually goes far beyond the money frontier; it also sets a boundary between church and state in the promotion of religious ideas. The Court, speaking through Justice Black, said:

> The "establishment of religion" clause of the First Amendment means at least this: Neither a state nor the federal government can set up a church. Neither can pass laws which aid one religion, aid all religions, or prefer one religion over another. Neither can force nor influence a person to go to or remain away from church against his will or force him to profess a belief or disbelief in any religion. No person can be punished for entertaining or professing religious beliefs or disbeliefs, for church attendance or non-attendance. No tax in any amount, large or small, can be levied to support any religious activities or institutions, whatever they may be called, or whatever form they may adopt to teach or practice religion. Neither a state nor the federal government can, openly or secretly, participate in the affairs of any religious organizations or groups and *vice versa*. In the words of Jefferson, the clause against establishment of religion by law was intended to erect "a wall of separation between church and state."

So much for the principles. This ringing pronouncement in favor of separation has blocked all use of tax funds for the central activities of sectarian schools, except in those few isolated centers of the Middle West where public schools have been taken over by Catholic religious orders. These captive schools are educational freaks and will certainly be wiped out when local taxpayers finally bring their existence to the attention of the Supreme Court.

The Court astonished some of its admirers in the Everson case by splitting five to four in applying its own principles to the border-line case of bus transportation. Was bus transportation at public expense a legitimate service to the child or an illegitimate service to the religious institution? The majority called the service legitimate and evolved a new "child welfare theory" to support it. Admitting that the use of public money for such transportation would help the sectarian schools maintain their attendance, the majority still argued that it was not a contribution to the schools as such but only an aid to "help parents get their children, regardless of their religion, safely and expeditiously to and from accredited schools." It classed such services with police protection.

In spite of this concession, the decision was far more of a victory than a defeat for believers in church–state separation. In effect, it legalized the use of public money in sectarian schools for such health and welfare services as school lunches and medical examinations, which nobody had opposed anyway. It sanctioned the use of public funds for school buses under the strictly limited conditions established by the New Jersey statute. But, by inference and dictum, it set a fairly clear limit to such use of public money, indicating that bus transportation was at the edge of the financial frontier. The warning was clear: thus far and no farther.

The Court also made it clear that its action on buses was purely permissive. The majority said specifically that a state *could* provide such services exclusively for public school pupils *if it wished*. Most of the states — twenty-eight out of fifty in 1959 — still refused to supply such services for sectarian schools, and some of those that nominally grant consent actually limit the services very strictly. Catholic authorities usually count only seventeen states as granting the privilege in reality. And states which have strict prohibitions against such a use of public funds have been left undisturbed. The Court has made no attempt to override their present laws providing public funds for public school pupils only, nor has it made any attempt to declare that free bus transportation for sectarian school children is a constitutional right rather than a legislative privilege.

Even this relatively small financial concession to sectarian schools was altogether too much for four of the justices in the Everson case —Jackson, Rutledge, Frankfurter and Burton. They considered the bus appropriation an illegal gift to the sectarian school, not a welfare grant to the child himself. Justice Rutledge wrote a brilliant historical analysis of the background of the First Amendment showing that it was designed to prevent "every form of public aid or support for religion." Jackson's dissent was an equally acute analysis of the position of the Catholic school in Catholicism, showing that the parish school is perhaps the "most vital" part of the Church itself, ordained by Canon Law and controlled entirely by the hierarchy. "The state," he said, "cannot maintain a Church and it can no more tax its citizens to furnish free carriage to those who attend a Church."

The question naturally arose: How much of this definitive new interpretation of the establishment clause of the First Amendment could and should be applied retroactively to all the past cases of public expenditures for religious institutions? Since the Court never answers such a question until a specific case is brought before it, one can only guess at the answer.

Probably the Court under the Everson doctrine would say that public grants to church hospitals are legitimate if distributed without denominational preference, but no one can say whether the justices would approve the use of public money for hospitals that insist on denominational medical codes. That question has never been raised in the highest tribunal since the Court began to handle the religion clauses of the Constitution analytically. Protestant and Jewish hospitals apparently have nothing to fear from the Everson bus ruling; Catholic hospitals might have, since they insist on a Catholic medical and surgical code for patients of all faiths. At present, denominational hospitals are getting many millions each year through the Hill–Burton Act under a Court decision of 1899, whose reasoning Judge Rutledge described in the Everson case opinion as "highly artificial."[4]

One current type of public expenditure for sectarian pupils in some states would seem to be invalidated by the Court's reasoning in the Everson bus case. That is the expenditure of public funds for non-religious textbooks for pupils in sectarian schools. Such expenditures for Louisiana's private school pupils were sanctioned as constitutional in 1930 by a court which did not even consider the application of the First Amendment to the situation.[5] If a textbook case ever reaches the Court again and is discussed on its merits, it is difficult to see how such use of public funds can be approved even under the child welfare theory. A textbook is not an article of health or safety equipment but a basic feature in the educational process itself.

Of course, *any* feature of a school system can be treated as a welfare service to individual children if judges care to stretch the child benefit concept to the point of absurdity. Transportation to Sunday school might be classed as a safety measure; even the teachers' uniforms and the blackboards on the walls might be crammed into that category. This is one reason why defenders of the separation of church and state regard the concession of bus funds in the Everson case as potentially dangerous. The amount of money involved is not large. The critical question is whether the child benefit theory will be stretched under ecclesiastical pressure to cover more than the Court intended.

The Catholic World, in an open letter to President Eisenhower in 1955, gave a dramatic illustration of the way in which the bus

---

[4] *Bradfield* v. *Roberts,* 175 U.S. 291 (1899).

[5] *Cochran* v. *Louisiana State Board,* 281 U.S. 370.

concession could be stretched.[6] Its editorial, entitled "Eisenhower and Parochial Schools," asked whether the federal government is "planning to offer any help toward the building of non–public schools" and declared that the "wall of separation said to have been erected by the First Amendment exists only in the mind or rather in the imagination of legal students smoking the opium of secularism." It continued:

> It's time to put a stop to such juggling of the meaning of a patently clear Amendment. . . . in the matter of the erecting of new school buildings, it's obvious that American children are entitled to the benefits of public welfare legislation regardless of race, creed or color. That was the decision of the United States Supreme Court in February 1947, upholding a New Jersey statute providing free bus transportation for children attending Catholic schools. American youths, whether Catholic, Protestant or Jewish, have a right to be educated in school buildings that have decent physical facilities. . . . there is nothing sectarian about heating equipment, windows and a roof over children's heads. . . .

When a sober religious journal takes such liberties with a Supreme Court decision, it is apparent that a Supreme Court justice's life is not a happy one. If he makes any concession to either side in a heated religious controversy over public money, his every word may be used as a verbal hand grenade on the sectarian barricades.

Religion in Public Schools

The financial challenge to the First Amendment in the Everson bus case was primarily a Catholic challenge. The religion-in-public-schools challenge was originally Protestant—and still is. Throughout the nation during the nineteenth century, some Protestant encroachments on the neutrality of the public school were condoned over the protests of Catholics, Jews and free-thinkers. These Protestant encroachments were a major factor in persuading the Catholic hierarchy to establish a separate and competing Catholic School system.

Beginning in 1913, a system of religious instruction, chiefly under Protestant auspices, had developed in connection with many public schools. It came to be known as the "released-time" system, operating sometimes in public school buildings, and sometimes in outside private buildings. Catholic leaders at first were hostile or indifferent to this system. Later they became its chief advocates and beneficiaries.

---

[6] *Catholic World* (April, 1955).

The issue of the constitutionality of this plan finally reached the Court in 1948. It was raised by a humanist, Mrs. Vashti McCollum of Illinois. The verdict handed down by the Court in this case was such a sweeping rebuke to all those who attempted to use public classrooms for religious education that it provoked much hostile comment in both Protestant and Catholic circles.

Terry McCollum, ten-year-old son of a professor at the University of Illinois, was compelled to sit alone in a Champaign public school once a week while other students in his class received religious instruction from a Protestant teacher who was brought into the school to teach religion. The class was taught on school time in Terry's regular classroom. There was a separate class in the basement for Catholic pupils.

Terry's mother, Vashti McCollum, objected to this procedure as a taxpayer and a parent on the ground that it was an illegal establishment of religion in a tax-supported institution. She carried her case to the United States Supreme Court at great expense, losing the vote of every judge in every lower court on the way. In the highest Court she won a resounding eight-to-one victory. The Court, with only Justice Reed dissenting, decided that all definite religious instruction as such should be eliminated from all public classrooms in America. Of course, the decision did not bar an objective treatment of religion in history or literature classes. It only barred the teaching of religion as sectarian promotion.

Both Justice Black, speaking for the Court, and Justice Frankfurter, in a concurring opinion, stressed the affirmative reasons for this decision. "For the First Amendment," said Justice Black, "rests upon the premise that both religion and government can best work to achieve their lofty aims if each is left free from the other within its respective sphere." Said Justice Frankfurter: "Separation means separation, not something less. Jefferson's metaphor in describing the relation between Church and State speaks of a 'wall of separation,' not of a fine line easily overstepped."

Justice Reed, in lonely dissent, declared: "The phrase 'an establishment of religion' may have been intended by Congress to be aimed only at a state church, not at aid to all churches." (This "multiple establishment" theory was and is the official theory of the Catholic Church.)[7] The Court disagreed with Reed and reaffirmed the posi-

---

[7] As stated by the Catholic bishops of the United States in "The Christian in Action," a long official pronouncement reprinted in full in the *New York Times* of November 21, 1948.

tion that the Constitution prohibits not only preferential aid to any one church but general aid to all churches. The justices were obviously astonished when the counsel for the state of Illinois argued before them that the state had a perfect right to distribute $5 million a year "to religion" so long as all faiths were treated alike.

Church and State—How High A Wall?*

Milton Himmelfarb and Ivan Shapiro

This selection consists of two articles: the first is by Milton Himmelfarb alone, and the second is a discussion between Ivan Shapiro and Himmelfarb occasioned by the earlier article. Himmelfarb is one of the contributing editors of *Commentary*, the magazine in which these articles appeared; Ivan Shapiro is a practicing attorney and is on the board of directors of the New York Civil Liberties Union.

[Statement — Himmelfarb]

The Jews are probably more devoted than anyone else in America to the separation of church and state. At times, hearing some of us talk about separation, or reading the statements of our organizations, one has the impression that we think ourselves more loyal to the Constitution and more skilled in its interpretation as well — although of course nobody ever says that in so many words. Thoughts protected against expression, as this one is, can be foolish. We are not more loyal to the Constitution or more skilled in its interpretation, we are only more separationist. And with every passing year our separationism comes closer to being part of the "old order" that Tennyson, in those verses that used to be so popular, wanted to see "yielding place to new;/ . . . Lest one good custom should corrupt the world."

The case for the regnant Jewish ideology or emotion goes this way: Granted, there must be something special in our own experience and memory, and some strong feeling about what is in our interest, to account for our separationist fervor; but we perceive and intend separation to be for the good of all as well as for our own good. Thirty years ago the Jews more than anyone else warned against Hitler and Nazism. Afterward, everybody could see that we had been right, that we had not merely been pleading our own cause when we said that resistance to Hitler and Nazism was not a Jewish in-

* Milton Himmelfarb, "Church and State: How High a Wall?," *Commentary* (July, 1966), 23–29; and Ivan Shapiro and Milton Himmelfarb, "Church and State," *Commentary* (December, 1966), 79–89. Reprinted from *Commentary* by permission; copyright © 1966 by the American Jewish Committee.

terest alone but the interest of all. Similarly now in church-and-state matters.

Because the Jews have had to pay for the lesson—so the case continues—we know that separation of church and state is good and the absence of separation is bad. A country with separation is democratic, tolerant, open, free; a country without separation is despotic, persecuting, closed, unfree. The greater the separation, as in America and France, the more democracy and tolerance; the less the separation, as in Spain, Tsarist Russia, and the Papal States before the unification of Italy, the less democracy and tolerance. Of course Jews do better in an America and a France than in a Spain and a Tsarist Russia. Doesn't everyone? In wanting America to be ever more separationist, which is to say ever more American, we want it to be ever better for all. "Religious freedom," in the words of the canon, "is most secure where church and state are separated, and least secure where church and state are united."

A good, strong case—or it would be if not for the vice of faulty enumeration. Where do you put England, Denmark, Norway, and Sweden, with their state churches? No one can deny that Great Britain and Scandinavia are free and democratic and that religious freedom is closer to being most secure there than least secure. Nor can any Jew deny that those countries are, as we used to say, good for the Jews. (Proportionately, more than seven times as many Jews are in the House of Commons as in the population of the United Kingdom.) On the other hand, in the Soviet Union church and state are constitutionally separate, but the Soviet Union is neither free nor democratic nor good for the Jews, and so far from making religious freedom secure—let alone most secure—it persecutes religion.

It may be argued that Soviet persecution does not fairly come under the head of separation and that state persecution of religion is a kind of negative mode of state establishment of religion. Without conceding the argument, let us return to the Soviet Union when we consider secularism and for the moment instead compare state–church England with separationist France. In democracy and freedom, the two are alike (or used to be, before de Gaulle's somewhat · authoritarian Fifth Republic); in openness and tolerance to Jews, the state–church country is better than the separationist one. Which is not to stay that establishment is better than separation, but only that other things—notably democracy as it is inclined by national culture and tradition—make the issue of separation/establishment quite secondary.

Only two years ago the Ecole Normale Supérieure, the nursery of the French intellectual elite, tried to keep out a qualified Jewish student because he observed the Sabbath. Why, he was asked, should he be admitted to an institution that trains *lycée* professors? A *lycée* has Saturday classes, like all state schools in France. Would not his Sabbath observance prevent him from teaching? The Ecole Normale Supérieure has been traditionally on the side of the French Revolution—republican, anti-clerical, anti-anti-Semitic— and since before the university careers of the Reinach brothers and Léon Blum, it has had Jewish students. But unlike the other Jewish students before him, this one was religious. Keeping in mind the distinction between secularist and religious Jews may help us to understand something about ourselves in the United States.

For a long time the distinction was blurred in the American Jewish community because in this country, church–state issues tend to be school issues. Our separationism goes back to the time when the public school was in many ways a common-denominator or inter-sectarian Protestant school. In that age of Protestant imperialism, as it has been called, the virtues and standards of America were so widely held to be the same as the virtues and standards of Protestantism that a public school had to be a basically Protestant school. One reason why the founder of American Reform Judaism, Isaac Mayer Wise, was a Copperhead in the Civil War was that he resented the Protestant imperialism of the abolitionists. (Lincoln needed the support of the Know-Nothings and did not condemn them publicly. Elijah Lovejoy, the abolitionist martyr, printed anti-Catholic tracts.) It was Wise who began the unbroken Reform tradition of opposing public school Protestantism in the name of separation. Whether he would have opposed religion-in-general in the schools is unclear. In Germany his masters and colleagues took it for granted that the state should favor religion.

Sometimes Wise's tradition was a well-kept secret among his disciples and successors, because the laity was in no mood to attract attention by protest; yet while Reform rabbis now disagree about God, Torah, and Israel, they still do not disagree about the separationist article of faith, though Protestant imperialism has gone the way of so many other imperialisms. And just as the Irish taught the rest of the Catholics how to be American, so Reform Judaism taught Orthodoxy and Conservatism. Separation became the common platform of the major varieties of Jewish religion in America. (The Orthodox have begun to go their own way, but that is a long story.)

Wise would have been happy with no Lord's Prayer in the schools, but only yesterday we were unhappy even with the Regents' prayer, certified desirable by the Lubavitcher Rebbe himself.

As for the Jewish secularists, they have opposed religion in the schools for a simple reason. They are secularists. For a secularist, religion is infantile and infantilizing, the enemy of enlightenment, science, progress, freedom, and peace. The less religion a society or community has, he says, the better it is.

But religionists and secularists do not live apart in the Jewish community. They have in common ideas and, above all, emotions. Few Jews of Central or East European origin or parentage, whether Orthodox or Reform, religious or secularist, have been able to think well of the church. The church was Pobedonostsev, with his vision of a third of the Jews of Russia converting, a third emigrating, and a third dying of hunger. The church was the threat of pogroms in the Easter season. The church was the Mortara case, the Dreyfus case, the Beilis case. "Christian" was part of the name an anti-Semitic party would give itself, in Protestant Prussia as in Catholic Austria. To Christians, Theodor Reik wrote when he still lived in Austria, Judaism was uncanny (mostly because of circumcision) and therefore fearsome. To Central and East European Jews, it was the iconic, sacramental, and sacerdotal Christianity they saw about them that was uncanny, and it still is to their children and grandchildren. Until a few years ago, the common memories and emotions and sense of danger tended to obscure the differences between Jewish religionists and secularists. So united was the Jewish front that only occasionally would a mainstream rabbi be bold enough to advise his confreres that they would do well, if only for the sake of public relations, to phrase their separationist statements in rather more religious-sounding language.

In Isaac Mayer Wise's Midwest, the Christian environment was Protestant. For most Jews today, who live in and near the great cities, the Christian environment is apt to be mainly Catholic. Wise's separationism was a defense against what he saw as a Protestant threat; ours is mostly against what we see as a Catholic threat, and especially what we see as the threat of the parochial school.

Traditions die hard, even the traditions of the untraditional. A man will say that the United States must rethink its foreign policy from beginning to end because the world has changed. Ask him to rethink his own policy because the world has changed and he will tell you he is no trimmer or opportunist; let the weaklings and conformists veer with the winds of popularity, he will remain loyal to his principles. Everyone thinks he is a dissenter and nonconformist—in good faith, because there are always communities of opinion and fashion in opposition to which he can honestly see himself as one. What he prefers to overlook is that there are also communities of opinion and fashion—or, more honorifically, of thought and style—to which he relates positively, and in that relation his nonconformity can be quite conformist. In our own community, the informal and private one or the organized and public one, separationism is not a bit nonconformist. (It is curious that dissent/dissenter, nonconformity/nonconformist should come to us from the language of English ecclesiastical history.)

As things are today, religionists and moderate secularists have one interest and radical separationists another, and our separationism now serves the radical interest. (Radical is generally not an O.K. word, but I cannot think of anything better. Extreme is even less O.K., consistent is not what I mean, and fanatical is insulting.) Whether a secularist is moderate or radical depends on whether his secularism is one of several more or less equal goods or whether it is his chief good; whether it is a means as well as an end, to be judged in part by its usefulness in furthering other ends, or whether it is more like an ultimate end. For the moderate, separationism is a strategy more than a philosophy, and if new conditions call for a change in strategy he will be ready to make the change. For the radical, the strategy goes so closely with the philosophy that change can only be betrayal. As integralist Catholics are convinced (notwithstanding Vatican II) that the marriage of Throne and Altar is God's will, so radical secularists are convinced that root-and-branch separationism is Reason's dictate.

What are the considerations that should induce a moderate secularist, and all the more a religionist, to question his inherited separationism? The first of these may by itself not be strictly probative, at least about America, but it points to something. For secularists the example of the Soviet Union should teach skepticism about the secularist faith itself. The Soviet Union is the most secularist society in what used to be Christendom (or Islam, Judaism never having secularist faith itself. The Soviet Union is the most secularist society separationism has gone so far as to become persecution of religion; and in that most secularist society, secularism is not the companion or handmaiden of freedom, intelligence, and all the other good things of man's mind and spirit, as secularists once thought it must be.

Rather it is the companion or handmaiden of the jailer of art and literature, science and scholarship and philosophy, honest thought and honest feeling. Not church–state England or Sweden vilifies and imprisons Brodsky, Sinyavsky, and Daniel, but the Soviet Union, which calls itself the guardian of enlightenment and the scourge of obscurantism. For a Jew it should also matter that nowhere else in what used to be Christendom are Jews and Judaism persecuted— alone among the Soviet nationalities, including the Germans, and more than the other Soviet religions.

In America a state church on the English or Swedish model is out of the question, and that is all the more reason why the separation decreed by the Constitution should be defended against mutation into separationism. For separationism can be tyrannical even here. No citizens of this country are more peaceful and inoffensive than the Amish, yet a few months ago agents of the Iowa public schools were photographed pursuing Amish children through the fields to drag them into schools that the parents had rejected for religious reasons. Not long after, in New York, it took a decision by the superintendent of schools himself to allow a high-school boy to cover his head in class. A Board of Education lawyer had ruled that if the boy wore a *kippah* he would be breaching the wall of separation between church and state! (The superintendent's name is Donovan.)

Almost as alarming is the growing isolation of Jewish separationism from the social liberalism of which it used to be part. On every side, President Johnson's aid-to-education and anti-poverty legislation is recognized as a major advance, and if liberals have a complaint, it is that the legislation does not go far enough. Liberal Protestants, accustomed to suspicion of Catholic designs on the public treasury and critical of Johnson on foreign policy, marvel at his achievement in bypassing the kinds of church–state objections —or rationalizations—that invariably killed similar bills in the past. The congressional opponents of Johnson's legislation, who went down continuing to profess indignation over the breach in the wall, were mostly reactionaries and racists.

Together with these stand the radical separationists, although theirs is a true and not a feigned indigation. They are unreconciled to educational benefits being extended to children in non-public (mostly Catholic parochial) schools, and to churches being included among appropriate neighborhood institutions for conducting anti-poverty programs. As the separationists see it, the child-benefit theory is a mere device for benefiting parochial schools by the back door while evading the (presumed) constitutional prohibition of benefits by the front door, and churches and church-related institutions have no business in anti-poverty programs or anything else that gets public money.

What if the benefits cannot readily be extended to children outside their non-public school? What if excluding a church or a church-related institution in this or that neighborhood weakens the effort to help the poor raise themselves out of poverty? Your singleminded separationist, after first trying to deny that your questions are real questions, can say nothing. Creditably, American liberalism in general does not accept this kind of hard-heartedness. The separationists make the usual defense in such cases: it is not really we who are hard-hearted but the other fellow, to whom we refuse to pay blackmail and who has maneuvered us into a false position. They may believe this, but whenever I hear or read Jewish separationists weighing the claim of the poor against the claim of separationism, their emotion goes to separationism. Yet we are still fond of thinking ourselves *rahamanim bene rahamanim,* the compassionate sons of compassionate fathers.

If not even regard for the poor moves the separationist to condone back-door dealings and aid, it is easy to imagine what he thinks about the front door. But here, too, his singlemindedness is beginning to isolate him. He cannot bring himself to look upon his favorite doctrine as one of many good things, not necessarily compatible in its fullness with the other good things in *their* fullness, and subject, like all of them, to compromise and give-and-take.

Of late some remarkable voices have been heard for governmental aid to the non-public school: the *New Republic* and Walter Lippmann, among others. Their purpose is not to help the Catholic schools but to help American education; or better, to help bring about the conditions in which all American can have the best possible education. Since the quality of the nation's life will depend so greatly on education, Lippmann and the others say, education has a more urgent claim on the nation than separationism. This means helping the Catholic schools, because so many children are educated there— about one in every seven. The Catholic schools need money, in quantities that can come only from government, to hire more teachers so that classes will be smaller, to get good teachers by paying good salaries, to improve classrooms, to build up libraries.

The First Amendment does not command, "Thou shalt not give governmental aid to parochial schools," it commands that there shall be no establishment of religion and no curtailment of the free exercise of religion. The rabbis said that the gates of interpretation of the Torah are not closed, and the Supreme Court has shown that neither are the gates of interpretation of the Constitution closed. If the justices think the nation needs education more than separationism, they can easily decide that the Constitution permits aid to nonpublic education. If they think otherwise, then it is the turn of the gates of amendment not to be closed. Having had an amendment prohibiting liquor and another anulling the prohibition, the Constitution can have an amendment allowing aid to religious or church-related schools.

This kind of talk is hardly daring any more, but to most separationists it is novel and perverse wickedness. That is not liberal open-mindedness. It is more like the outrage of a nineteenth-century, Herbert Spencer liberal confronted with the immoral proposal that the government should take taxes from him to support a school for educating his neighbor's children. There are still such liberals, only for many years now they have been called, by general agreement, reactionaries.

To Jews, Jewish separationists like to say that separationism is necessary for our safety and well-being. I think this argument is a second thought, invoked to justify a decision already taken on another ground. Those who invoke it remind me of a businessman who wants to contribute corporation money to a university or a community chest or the symphony orchestra. Possibly he wants to do it because he is a decent, generous man, but he has to justify his decency, to himself as well as to the other officers and the stockholders, by giving businesslike reasons for the contribution; it will be good for public relations, or it will help to make the environment so healthy that the corporation will be able to thrive.

There would be nothing wrong about consulting our interest when we are making up our minds whether to support governmental aid to church schools in the name of better education or to oppose it in the name of separation. If we consulted interest, we would estimate advantages and disadvantages by applying the appropriate calculus. That is how a man runs his business, or he is soon out of business. It is how Mr. McNamara chooses between missiles and manned bombers, submarines and aircraft carriers. But though I follow the Jewish discussions, I recall little that resembles a true weighing of alternatives. We prefer incantatory repetition of the dogma that separationism is our interest.

It is time we actually weighed the utility and cost of education against the utility and cost of separationism. All the evidence in America points to education, more than anything else, influencing adherence to democracy and egalitarianism. All the evidence points to Catholic parochial education having the same influence. (And all the evidence points to Catholic anti-Semitism as no greater than Protestant, and possibly less.) Something that nurtures a humane, liberal democracy is rather more important to Jews than 24-karat separationism.

There is another thing related to the Catholic parochial schools that we ought to weigh in the balance of Jewish interest. Consensus has become a dirty word on the Left and among intellectuals. In parts of the world suffering either from despotism or from chaos, they must envy America for this additional sign of affluence, that here people can afford to depreciate consensus. Outside the American consensus stand the far Right and the anti-Semites. (There is anti-Semitism on the outside Left, too, and among some of the young Jews in it.) It is good to broaden the consensus, to bring inside those who are outside. They change when they come inside.

Why are some people outside? Usually because they have a grievance. They feel they are disregarded and treated unfairly. The sociologists call this feeling ressentiment; let us call it sullenness. When statesmanship becomes aware that a social group is sullen, it tries to remove the causes, if that can be done without unacceptable cost to the other participants in the competitive cooperation of political society. In part it is because the Negroes have finally been seen to be sullen, in this sense, that the government is trying to make room for them in the game and bring them into the consensus. Sometimes, of course, a group's price for giving up its sullenness is too high for everybody else, and it has to be left outside—like the Birchers, who just for a start want the political and social game to return to the rules of the 1920's or the 1890's. But it must be conceded that some people, disoriented and bewildered by the passing of the America they were comfortable in, are needlessly being driven into the Radical Right. Some good libertarians are saying that such symbolic victories for separationism as making Bible reading in the schools illegal have been won at too high a real cost—the sullenness of the defeated and the departure of some of them from the consensus.

Many Catholics are sullen. For a non-Catholic it should not be unreasonably arduous to pretend for a moment that he has children in a parochial school. Call it role-playing. For the average Catholic, affluence is either a figure of speech or what someone else has: he is less affluent than the average Episcopalian, Congregationalist, or Jew. The taxes he pays to the public schools keep rising. So do his parochial-school costs, but the parochial school continues to fall behind the public school—in the size of classes, in salaries to attract good teachers, in equipment and amenities. He can hardly afford to pay once, but he has to pay twice; and in return his children get an education that he fears may not be good enough. This, when the diploma society is already here and meritocracy is on the horizon, and when his children's chances of making it depend more than ever on the education he can give them.

He asks for aid, and a coalition of Protestants and Jews, far from respecting him for having done the hard thing so long, answer coldly that private education must be paid for privately; if he can't afford it, let him not complain, let him use the public schools. At the same time he sees that in the cities many in the coalition, whether pants manufacturers or intellectuals, do indeed pay to send their children to private schools. Apparently they believe non-public education is like a Cadillac: just as it would be ridiculous to subsidize a poor man's purchase of a Cadillac, so it would be to subsidize his purchase of non-public education. He suspects that this uncharacteristic enthusiasm of theirs for the principles of Ayn Rand is due rather to their distaste for Catholic education specifically than for non-public education generally.

Then, in self-defense, or out of resentment, or as a means of exerting pressure, the Catholic votes against higher taxes for the public schools, and the coalition is confirmed in its opinion of him. He is narrow-minded. But, tolerant and understanding, and proud of it, they tell each other that it isn't really his fault. It is the priests who make him send his children to the parochial school, the priests who make him sullen about the inevitable, unalterable consequences. *We* do not need a priest to make us prefer a non-public school, only *he* does. Tell them of the evidence that the average Catholic parent prefers the parochial school of his own accord; they answer: never heard of it, propaganda. If I were that Catholic parent, I could be pretty sullen.

Catholics, therefore, have a real grievance. To remove the grievance would be just. It would also be statesmanlike, and would help to improve the education of a significant part of the American population. People are coming to see that. In the past few years the in a parochial school. Call it role-playing. For the average Catholic, affluence is either a figure of speech or what someone else has: he is less affluent than the average Episcopalian, Congregationalist, or Jew. The taxes he pays to the public schools keep rising. So do his parochial-school costs, but the parochial school continues to fall behind the public school—in the size of classes, in salaries to attract good teachers, in equipment and amenities. He can hardly afford to pay once, but he has to pay twice; and in return his children get an education that he fears may not be good enough. This, when the diploma society is already here and meritocracy is on the horizon, and when his children's chances of making it depend more than ever on the education he can give them.

He asks for aid, and a coalition of Protestants and Jews, far from respecting him for having done the hard thing so long, answer coldly that private education must be paid for privately; if he can't afford it, let him not complain, let him use the public schools. At the same time he sees that in the cities many in the coalition, whether pants manufacturers or intellectuals, do indeed pay to send their children to private schools. Apparently they believe non-public education is like a Cadillac: just as it would be ridiculous to subsidize a poor man's purchase of a Cadillac, so it would be to subsidize his purchase of non-public education. He suspects that this uncharacteristic enthusiasm of theirs for the principles of Ayn Rand is due rather to their distaste for Catholic education specifically than for non-public education generally.

Then, in self-defense, or out of resentment, or as a means of exerting pressure, the Catholic votes against higher taxes for the public schools, and the coalition is confirmed in its opinion of him. He is narrow-minded. But, tolerant and understanding, and proud of it, they tell each other that it isn't really his fault. It is the priests who make him send his children to the parochial school, the priests who make him sullen about the inevitable, unalterable consequences. *We* do not need a priest to make us prefer a non-public school, only *he* does. Tell them of the evidence that the average Catholic parent prefers the parochial school of his own accord; they answer: never heard of it, propaganda. If I were that Catholic parent, I could be pretty sullen.

Catholics, therefore, have a real grievance. To remove the grievance would be just. It would also be statesmanlike, and would help to improve the education of a significant part of the American population. People are coming to see that. In the past few years the

It is time we actually weighed the utility and cost of education against the utility and cost of separationism. All the evidence in America points to education, more than anything else, influencing adherence to democracy and egalitarianism. All the evidence points to Catholic parochial education having the same influence. (And all the evidence points to Catholic anti-Semitism as no greater than Protestant, and possibly less.) Something that nurtures a humane, liberal democracy is rather more important to Jews than 24-karat separationism.

There is another thing related to the Catholic parochial schools that we ought to weigh in the balance of Jewish interest. Consensus has become a dirty word on the Left and among intellectuals. In parts of the world suffering either from despotism or from chaos, they must envy America for this additional sign of affluence, that here people can afford to depreciate consensus. Outside the American consensus stand the far Right and the anti-Semites. (There is anti-Semitism on the outside Left, too, and among some of the young Jews in it.) It is good to broaden the consensus, to bring inside those who are outside. They change when they come inside.

Why are some people outside? Usually because they have a grievance. They feel they are disregarded and treated unfairly. The sociologists call this feeling ressentiment; let us call it sullenness. When statesmanship becomes aware that a social group is sullen, it tries to remove the causes, if that can be done without unacceptable cost to the other participants in the competitive cooperation of political society. In part it is because the Negroes have finally been seen to be sullen, in this sense, that the government is trying to make room for them in the game and bring them into the consensus. Sometimes, of course, a group's price for giving up its sullenness is too high for everybody else, and it has to be left outside—like the Birchers, who just for a start want the political and social game to return to the rules of the 1920's or the 1890's. But it must be conceded that some people, disoriented and bewildered by the passing of the America they were comfortable in, are needlessly being driven into the Radical Right. Some good libertarians are saying that such symbolic victories for separationism as making Bible reading in the schools illegal have been won at too high a real cost—the sullenness of the defeated and the departure of some of them from the consensus.

Many Catholics are sullen. For a non-Catholic it should not be unreasonably arduous to pretend for a moment that he has children no other means of communication. Now we have electronic media, and above all radio and television, which influence opinion probably more than print. In our time unhindered communication of opinion and information depends on a freedom of the press that includes freedom of radio and TV. But the relation of government to radio and TV has to be totally different from its relation to the printing press.

The libertarian's conception of the ideal relation of government to the press is that there shall be no relation at all: government and press have nothing to do with each other, nobody needs a license to publish. In principle there is no limit to the number of newspapers or presses. With radio and TV, on the other hand, the laws of physics impose a limit. Two stations cannot operate on the same wavelength at the same time in the same place, so someone must determine that A shall operate and B shall not. That is, the government; and it is to government that A and B come to plead for a license. A government that respects freedom of the press finds itself having to license the radio-and-TV part of the press. What would Jefferson have thought?

In deciding whether to license A or B, the government has first to decide which of the two will probably better serve the public interest and the needs of society. But these include religion in its many forms. Consequently, when the government examines the record of a radio or TV licensee it must ask, among other things, how he has served his community's religious interests and needs. If it did not ask this question, if it asked everything else but not this, a licensee could exclude religion entirely from his programs; or give his own sect a monopoly of the time he allowed for religion; or set aside all that time for attacking a religion he disliked, or some religions, or religion in general; or sell all of it to the highest bidders. Yet a friend of mine considers that the government's asking about the religious programming of licensees breaches the wall of separation:[2]

> While the U.S. Supreme Court has been gradually strengthening Jefferson's "wall of separation between church and state," the Federal Communications Commission has been doing its best to persuade people to go to church. . . . The commission has held . . . that the proposed religious programming of one applicant for a television station . . . was superior to another because it afforded "a more positive proposal for providing time to diverse religious faiths." In another case, it gave a comparative—although not a

---

[2] Marcus Cohn, "Religion and the FCC," *Reporter* (January 14, 1965).

disqualifying—demerit to . . . [a] proposed program schedule [because it] failed to include "any strictly religious programs" and thus left a "void in . . . over-all program structure."

Radio and TV are not the instruments of the state, they are the instruments of society. The state is there, has to be there, only because a technology Jefferson could not dream of has made rationing the airwaves necessary. If Cohn's principle were followed, the FCC would not be protecting the separation of church and state, as he thinks. It would be promoting the separation of religion and society —something else again.

The late Theodore Leskes, a lamented colleague and an authority on First Amendment questions, was rather more convinced than I of the need for a wall. Nevertheless, when I asked him whether he objected to military chaplains, he answered that he could not object in principle. The army, he said, is a surrogate society. When the army drafts a man it is obligated to make available to him, insofar as possible, what he has had in the civilian life from which it cuts him off — including the opportunity for religious worship and guidance. Otherwise the government's maintenance of a conscript army would mean the government's exclusion of religion from the lives of some millions of young men.

And so with education. As late as the end of the nineteenth century President Garfield could say that a college education was a log with Mark Hopkins at one end and a student at the other. If no longer entirely true when he said it, it still had a certain verisimilitude. Now it would be absurd—not only about our colleges, but also about our high, junior high, and even elementary schools. These demand ever more costly laboratories, closed-circuit TV, equipment for teaching languages, psychological testing, vocational guidance.

When logs were cheap, it was rather widely possible to maintain non-public schools of the same quality as the public schools, even without governmental aid. Not any more. No violation of the First Amendment is needed to reduce freedom of the press substantively, by the disappearance of one paper after another; the only thing needed is for economic law to be allowed free play. Allowed free play, economic law would have the same effect on the non-public schools, but with an even worse effect on society. The space once occupied by non-public education would not be left empty. It would be filled by something we might call uniformitarianism, to coin an ugly word for describing an ugly condition.

In the political and social thought that has least to apologize for, despotism is understood to prevail when state and society are all but identical, when the map of the state can almost be superimposed on the map of society. In contrast, freedom depends on society's having loci of interest, affection, and influence besides the state. It depends on more or less autonomous institutions mediating between the naked, atomized individual and the state—or rather, keeping the individual from nakedness and atomization in the first place. In short, pluralism is necessary.

Given that a shriveling of the non-public must fatally enfeeble pluralism, especially in education; and given that the agent of that enfeeblement is the unchecked operation of economic law, the remedy is simple: check it. Let the govenment see that money finds its way to the non-public schools, so that they may continue to exist side by side with the public schools. That will strengthen pluralism, and so, freedom.

Arguments for non-governmental pluralism have to overcome the obstacle of their popularity with conservative immobilists. From Social Security to Medicare, an unfeeling Right has been quick to warn that the omnicompetent state is upon us. Nobody listens any more, the boy has cried wolf too often. But in the fable a real wolf finally appeared, and for us the state coextensive with society may yet appear. Technology encourages it. The simple fact that there are now so many people encourages it. The time when the state took little of the room of a man's life is gone. Happily, a man can favor the welfare state and still oppose the omnicompetent state.

Can government be expected to subsidize the non-public sector, to pay for keeping vigorously alive centers of influence and power whose very existence will limit its own influence and power? If government is democratic, the expectation is altogether realistic. American governments routinely subsidize the non-public sector: the deductibility provision in the federal and state income taxes is nothing but an indirect subsidy to non-public institutions—community chests, universities, theological seminaries, churches and synagogues. And a most reassuring thing about the poverty program is that government actually calls into being and finances civic grouping of the poor in order that they may make trouble for government—reassuring, because it shows democratic government understands that democracy requires government to have cooperators–rivals.

Historically, establishment has gone with monarchy: throne and altar, crown and mitre. Separation has gone with a republic: no king, no bishop. And in fact England, Denmark, Norway, and Sweden have established churches and are monarchies. Republicanism was once even more of a fighting creed than separation, but who in Great Britain or Scandinavia is excited by republicanism any longer? It has become an irrelevance, an anachronism. While monarchies have shown that they can be decent and democratic, republics have shown that they can be neither. In America separationism may soon be just as anachronistic, if only because our establishmentarians are not much more numerous than our monarchists.

Even the rhetoric is coming down with mustiness. "Wall of separation" may have sounded good once, but if you say it to a young man now he is as likely as not to think you mean the wall that separates Berlin. Leave it to a poet: "Something there is that doesn't love a wall."

[Debate — Shapiro and Himmelfarb]

IVAN SHAPIRO:

In his article in the July *Commentary*, Milton Himmelfarb took up arms against the principle of complete separation of church and state, and in particular against the prohibition of public aid to parochial schools. He charged his Jewish readers with being "radical separationists." Surely, he urged, they should at least favor state–church cooperation in the fields of education and social welfare. Mr. Himmelfarb advanced most of the arguments by which the Catholic Church and some rabbis (particularly, although not exclusively, Orthodox) have recently succeeded in procuring tens of millions of public dollars for parochial schools—a success which has been achieved in the face of considerable public opposition and constitutional proscription. Mr. Himmelfarb's arguments, therefore, warrant our close attention. I will attempt to examine here both the doctrine of separation of church and state and some of its applications, and I hope to show that continued adherence to strict separation is essential to the freedom of us all.

Let me make it clear that by the term "strict separation" I mean that no level of authority, from federal government to village hall, may either:

(1) Interfere with or coerce any church, or all churches, or any group declaring itself a religious body, in the fulfillment of its religious functions; or

(2) Support, through the use of public money, property, or

influence, any church, or all churches, or any denominationally controlled institution; or hold or favor any viewpoint concerning theological matters, however generalized or popular that viewpoint may be.

The first aspect of separation—insuring freedom from governmental interference—is now protected from federal, state, and local violation through the "free exercise of religion" clause of the First Amendment of the U.S. Constitution,[3] as well as through similar provisions in almost every state constitution.

The second aspect—barring governmental support of religion—is the one which is presently being debated. It is, of course, affirmed by the "establishment" clause of the First Amendment, and by the constitutions or judicial opinions of almost every state; but since the relevant provisions in the state constitutions are not identical to the First Amendment, it is sometimes the case that a given form of public assistance which has been declared lawful under the First Amendment may still be unlawful under a particular state constitution.

Many people (including Mr. Himmelfarb) proclaim themselves in favor of the abstract idea of separation, but abandon this position when the problem of specific applications arises. For some, the "necessary" exception to the principle is taken to be the issue of allowing prayers to be read in schools, or dismissing some pupils early so that they may receive separate religious instruction. Others would permit the wall of separation to be breached in order to provide children attending parochial schools with textbooks, TV sets, and publicly paid teachers. Still others, who would normally insist that the wall remain absolutely solid, nevertheless go about arranging special public favors for their churches, such as legislation authorizing them to conduct gambling games on church premises. One could go on listing such alleged "necessary exceptions" to the principle and still not list them all. Needless to say, if all the exceptions were openly countenanced by the courts (most have never been adjudicated), religion and government would no longer be separated; they would be living in lawful cohabitation.

Here we are at the source of the confusion about the meaning of "separation": it consists in lumping libertarian separationism with the traditional basis of Protestant support for separation. Historically, the Protestant idea has been that while government

---

[3] "Congress shall make no law respecting an establishment of religion, or prohibiting the free exercise thereof. . . ."

has no right to control either the churches or individual freedom of conscience, the government should nevertheless enforce the moral and spiritual values of Protestantism, suppressing "immorality" and inculcating Christian principles. This position derives mainly from the evangelical, anti-rationalist theological views held by left-wing Protestants in the seventeenth and eighteenth centuries. By contrast, the libertarian viewpoint, which derives from eighteenth-century rationalism, does not regard government as an instrument for the enforcement of religious values. The difference between the two positions is the difference between non-sectarian and secular government. To most separationist Protestants, the ideal state is non-sectarian, and remains neutral *vis-à-vis* competing Protestant sects, but is also actively committed to furthering the Protestant way of life. To libertarians, such theocratic views are hardly "separationist." Indeed, they are possible only in a country in which the power of the state is in the hands of Protestants.

If my own position is still unclear, let me openly state that I am a libertarian and one of those whom Mr. Himmelfarb chastises for being "radical separationists." My views are not part of my inheritance, but have been formed by many factors: my strong belief in freedom for every individual, as guaranteed by our Bill of Rights; the conclusions I have drawn, from my reading of history, about the woeful fate of individual freedom under conditions of active cooperation between religion and government; and my thinking about the means by which both individual liberty and the Great Society can be achieved in a democratic order.

I am a separationist because individual freedom—by which I mean the freedom to express unpopular thoughts and to act reasonably upon them without being punished and without losing the rights and opportunities available to those holding more popular views—cannot exist in any society in which particular theological attitudes are supported by public officials. I take it as a truism that governmental support of religion indicates a decision by the majority to endorse and foster publicly whatever common theological denominator links the beneficiaries of such support. The theology may entail as little as a belief in a Supreme Being, but so long as the will of the majority officially supports persons and organizations holding such a belief—while withholding identical support from non-believing or "other-believing" persons and organizations—the freedom of the society as a whole has been diminished. The non-believer is punished by receiving unequal treatment. Moreover, the believers themselves must know that the moment they cease being part of the majority, or lose its favor, they too will suffer a loss of freedom and equality.

There is no issue on which mankind has had longer or worse experience than the effects of cooperation between religion and government: one recalls the persecutions, disabilities, and absence of religious freedom in ancient Egypt, Orthodox Russia, and the Puritan Massachusetts Bay Colony. In our own time we observe that even in America, where we do not have a formal bond between church and state, a person may have to lie or perform a criminal act in order to buy a contraceptive, procure an abortion, or obtain a divorce, for the sole reason that the state government is enforcing theological doctrines. I find it abhorrent that I may be prevented by a state movie censor from seeing a film solely because some clergyman has deemed it hostile to his group. From endless examples, I have concluded that wherever government supports religion, by lending either its power or its wealth, individual freedom is impaired or destroyed.

"But," say the cooperationists, "you have pointed mainly to situations in which a single religion won the favor of the government. We too are opposed to that. What we want is for government to extend aid to *all* religions. In that way no single religion will have too much power." This is not true. My liberty would be equally impaired if the rabbis joined with the bishops to induce the state to ban *The Miracle* in exchange for the bishops' using their influence to have *The Merchant of Venice* or *Oliver Twist* removed from high-school reading lists. It did not lessen the harassment of Jehovah's Witnesses that they were equally offensive to Catholics, Protestants, and Jews.

Moreover, when cooperationists declare that the government should help all religions, I doubt whether they really want the government to extend its secular embrace to Black Muslims, Zen Buddhists, and each of the thousands of store-front evangelical churches. I rather suspect that cooperationists want the government to help only the few major religions which have been around long enough or have enough followers to have assumed "respectable" positions. But once we start selecting beneficaries and determining the status of a particular religion, we have launched ourselves on the course of repression, for unless we allow every group of two or more decide for itself whether it is a religion, we must set qualifications. If our standard is a belief in God or a

Supreme Being, we will exclude Buddhists, Humanists, Ethical Culturists, and others right from the start. If our standard is narrower, we will exclude still others. Later, as one or another of the "qualified" religions becomes more powerful (with the help of the public aid it receives), the way may be opened for it to exert greater control over the government, since it will no longer have to "play ball" with the other churches.

The history of the English Puritans provides a good illustration of this pattern. In 1630, they were a despised minority. Then they were able to make common cause with other sects. By 1650, they had control of the government, and became the persecutors of their former cohorts. It is too often the case that members of a religion who adhere strongly to their faith regard all others as schismatics, God-deniers, or otherwise unenlightened enemies. When the favor of government is bestowed upon a powerful and devout church, we have the stuff of which inquisitions, crusades, and pogroms are made.

The libertarian view of the relationship between religion and government is now, with some exceptions, the law throughout the country. This has partly been the result of a series of cases, starting in 1940, in which the Supreme Court of the United States has reinterpreted in a separationist light the twin commands of the First Amendment that "Congress shall make no law respecting an establishment of religion, or prohibiting the free exercise thereof. . . ." The Court has ruled, for instance, on the basis of its reading of the "free exercise" clause, that children whose religious scruples dictate otherwise cannot be compelled to salute a flag during a school program, and that no child can be compelled to recite or even listen to a prayer in school. It has also held that local governments cannot forbid the distribution of religious tracts in the streets, or require public officials to believe in God. Similarly, the Court has found that the "establishment" clause prohibits the states and the federal government from aiding religious practices and institutions. Thus, a state cannot allow clergymen to give instruction in public schools to pupils seeking such instruction, nor may public officials compose non-denominational prayers—however vapid—for public use. There have, of course, been exceptions in the actual decisions: Sunday Laws, released-time programs, and the spending of public money to provide transportation for children attending parochial schools, have been sustained as not violating the "establishment" clause. But even in cases such as these, the principles expressed by the Court have been largely separationist ones.

However, the current legal status of separation is only partly the result of Supreme Court decisions, although the Supreme Court today receives most of the blame (or credit) of this state of affairs. We frequently overlook the fact that for over a century almost all the states have been enforcing separationist policies, especially in matters of education, in response to the widespread popular demand for a democratic and secular government. The constitutions of most states have for a long time now explicitly forbidden any public assistance to schools and other institutions under sectarian control, and almost invariably the supreme courts of the few states which did not have such a constitutional proscription have read one into the existing law. Indeed, the Supreme Court seems to have entered the field at a relatively late date, and, by the standards of the laws of many states, has tolerated sectarian incursions beyond the permissible point.

When we turn to consider the "necessary exceptions" to the doctrine of separation urged by Mr. Himmelfarb, we realize that since 1964 the significance of the dispute has been magnified by the availability of enormous amounts of federal funds to parochial schools. The Economic Opportunity Act, which launched the war against poverty, provided that its programs were to be developed and administered by private, non-profit organizations (including churches), acting with public agencies. In 1965 came the Federal Elementary and Secondary Education Act, which expressly required that certain programs and facilities be made available equally to parochial and public-school pupils. Both statutes embody programs of the utmost importance to the nation, programs which have been urged by liberals for years. It is now apparent that the federal government alone has sufficient resources to attack successfully the nationwide problem of poverty and the lack of adequate educational opportunities. In prior years, resistance to the enactment of such legislation had been successfully led by segregationists, economic and social conservatives, and representatives of certain churches. The first two groups were finally outvoted and outmaneuvered. Unfortunately, the churches proved a more formidable barrier: the price exacted for the passage of the legislation was church participation in the new government programs.

Nevertheless, both the Economic Opportunity Act and the Federal Elementary and Secondary Education Act should provide benefits to all disadvantaged persons, regardless of their faith or color. The intention of both statutes was that the funds would be administered in a non-sectarian manner at publicly-owned facilities open to all—so that, for instance, children enrolled at parochial schools could participate with public-school children in after-school programs, or use the expanded libraries of the public schools. Similarly, it was expected that disadvantaged pre-school children, regardless of their faith, would participate in neighborhood "Operation Headstart" programs. Tragically, programs such as these have been boycotted by certain churches, which in some instances have even succeeded in inducing local officials to set up programs on church-controlled premises, for the exclusive benefit of the members of that church. Because these statutes are so new, there have as yet been no judicial interpretations.

Mr. Himmelfarb, like other proponents of public aid to church-controlled schools and institutions, invokes both negative and positive argument to support his view. The negative attack begins with the claim that separationism goes hand in hand with irreligion, godlessness, and Soviet tyranny. It then laments that separationists are today isolating themselves from liberal social policies, such as those embodied in the 1964 and 1965 federal acts mentioned above. Next, it charges that refusing public aid to church institutions is a form of discrimination, and among other things, results in double taxation of a portion of the public. Finally, separationists are charged with isolating from the national consensus that portion of the citizenry which does not believe in separation, namely the Catholic community.

On the positive side, the critics argue that providing a "proper" education for pupils attending parochial schools is a more important social objective than keeping government and religion apart. Similarly, it is good public policy to broaden the consensus by bringing into our national life those groups which have placed themselves outside it. Finally, a constitutional argument is made: while aid to parochial schools and other sectarian agencies may be unlawful, these critics maintain, it is perfectly proper to give aid to the *children* who attend parochial schools. Let us consider first the negative arguments.

It is foolish to suggest that those fighting to maintain separation are principally interested in destroying religion. To be sure, many non-believers favor separation, but now, as in the past, the greatest advocates of separation of church and state have been religious leaders and the more devout among their followers. Principally, it has been the various Protestant churches—especially the Baptists and Unitarians—which have been opposed to mingling church and state and which have fought hardest to defend the wall of separation in the face of recent legislation. These Protestant groups have usually regarded public aid as a threat to the freedom of their churches; they feel that the government will inevitably obtain some measure of control over the recipient.

This is a point which has generally been ignored by the critics of separation, among whom it is common practice to ascribe American Protestant separationism solely to a prejudice against Catholics. But in fact, the separationist attitude was developed decades before the Catholic Church became a significant force in the United States. Protestant groups which are now endeavoring to find common theological ground with Catholics and others remain as committed to separation as ever.

Mr. Himmelfarb fears that by remaining separationists, Jews will find themselves opposing the progressive social attitudes embodied in some of the Great Society legislation. Yet even Mr. Himmelfarb acknowledges that this is a curious argument. It assumes that liberal social policies cannot be accomplished in a constitutional manner. It presents the triumph of "ultimatum" thinking: a person wants to achieve a liberal end, and is confronted by someone saying, "I may like what you are trying to do, but I won't let you do it unless you pay me"; the liberal is then castigated for objecting. I am not sure how Mr. Himmelfarb succeeded in turning the blackmailer into the virtuous party here, but that is indeed his position.

The truth is that it was the liberals who fought for years to win federal aid for education and a federal anti-poverty program; at every step of the way they were confronted and blocked by special-interest groups. On the local level this same struggle is reenacted annually in many Eastern suburbs when school-bond issues come to a vote. There is nothing in our democratic system to prevent churches or any other body from lobbying and voting for or against anything. But it does no credit to the cooperationists or their position to cast the rest of us in the villain's role when we refuse to go along with their unlawful requests. This suggests Orwellian "doublethink."

The contention that parents who elect parochial education for their children pay a double tax is another example of ill-considered reasoning. Let us realize that a church does not (in this country) have a legally enforceable power to tax anyone. Whatever it receives from its members comes in the form of voluntary gifts. And while we have made education compulsory, we have constitutionally guaranteed the right of parents to send their children to qualified non-public schools of their own choosing. Attendance at a prochial school is a matter of private choice, no different legally from giving a child private music lessons or sending him to summer camp. No law requires churches to maintain separate schools, or children to attend them. Many taxpayers do not use the public facilities for which they pay taxes (some, like parents of parochial-school children, because they choose not to; others, such as corporations, because they are not capable of going to school or entering a hospital). Similarly, bachelors and childless couples pay school taxes without ever expecting to derive a direct benefit.

Professor George LaNoue of Teachers College, Columbia University, has pointed out that a true "double-tax" argument can be made if public funds are used for the benefit of parochial schools: no taxpayer has a legal right to send his child to a particular parochial school, nor to vote for the persons who decide its educational policies. Public aid to parochial schools necessarily forces *every* taxpayer to support two school systems, one of which represents, and exists for the benefit of, only a portion of the community.

The fact that Mr. Himmelfarb sees the Catholic community as being outside the national consensus is also surprising, especially since the 1960 election, and most especially in view of the fact that most large Northern and Eastern cities are ruled by Catholics. Except on the issue of aid to parochial schools, I doubt whether Catholics themselves feel alienated or resentful. So far as the advocates of public aid are concerned, the parochial-school issue represents purely and simply a question of money. Their standing as Americans is not in question, and undoubtedly is not felt by them to be an issue.

Virtually everyone who supports the giving of public aid to parochial schools argues that it is good social policy to provide a "proper" education for these children. Such persons obviously assume that the education provided by the parochial schools is inadequate. This may or may not be the case. It is certainly true that many parochial-school administrators have confessed that parochial education, at least with respect to many of the parochial education, at least with respect to many of the non-theological courses, is inadequate. To the extent that this inadequacy is real, we must deplore the fact. A good education is vital to every individual, regardless of his faith or his economic status. But it is for this very reason that we are concerned with improving the public schools. After all, only the free public school is accessible to children of all colors, faiths, and economic levels. Here we come to the most critical "practical" consideration of the parochial-school issue: the fact that just when we have acknowledged the overwhelming need to improve our public schools, certain members of the community are seeking to divert a portion of the funds which have been provided for that purpose.

For example: under the 1965 federal act, $65 million is now available to New York State for books and certain facilities and services. Everyone acknowledges that this sum is not sufficient to meet the needs of the 3,200,000 children attending the public schools in this state, most of whom cannot afford private education. Nevertheless, New York has felt compelled under the federal law to allocate $15 million of this sum to the parochial schools, which now enroll 800,000 pupils, most of whose parents pay tuition or make substantial tax-deductible "contributions" to the church. In New York City, federal funds are being used to establish programs for parochial-school children which are not even available to public-school children. If this nation is to continue to honor its commitment to public education, it cannot afford to divert any of its funds to building up a rival sectarian system of schools. If churches desire to create private-school systems, they have no claim upon the public to support these schools. They must learn to give adequate support to their schools by themselves. A number of those churches which cry loudest for tax support have access to enormous amounts of money. Since the education and religious indoctrination of the young is of the greatest importance of the churches, it would seem that they could make greater efforts toward financing their schools adequately.

The argument in favor of public aid always stresses the fact that the particular form of aid given will be directed only toward the secular aspects of the education. That is, if books are provided, they will be books on physical science, mathematics, languages, and the like. Similarly, public-school teachers assigned to parochial schools will teach art, music, or remedial reading.

Cooperationists do not like being reminded that every church dollar saved from buying books or equipment, or from paying a teacher's salary, can be used to further the school's purely religious aims. No one, moreover, has raised the question whether parochial schools are capable of imparting a truly secular education. Why, after all, have the various religions established their own full-time schools, rather than teaching the matters which are of special concern to them on a part-time basis as a private supplement to the public-school curriculum? The answer, of course, it that the religious bodies which maintain full-time parochial schools believe that every aspect of education is, and must be, sectarian. Every subject taught in a full-time parochial school should be permeated by the doctrines of the sponsoring church. Thus, the papal encyclical, "Christian Education of Youth," issued in 1930, states that for the Catholic parochial schools, "it is necessary that all the teaching and the whole organization of the school, and its teachers, syllabus, and textbooks, in every branch, be regulated by the Christian spirit." The Lutherans hold the same view, and Jewish *yeshivot* and Greek Orthodox schools are founded upon a similar philosophy. Indeed, almost all religions regard total parochial education as the foundation stone of the entire religion. There is no question of their constitutional right to do so. It is, however, equally clear that they cannot at the same time claim to be giving secular instruction.

In their attempt to circumvent the constitutional prohibitions, parochial schools have developed the "child-benefit" theory. They point out, quite correctly, that while aid to the religious institution may be unlawful, public benefits afforded to children must include all children, and cannot exclude those who have elected to receive parochial education. Few libertarians would deny, for instance, that if all children are required to receive a smallpox vaccination from a public nurse during school hours, public nurses must also be stationed in parochial schools to administer the vaccine to the pupils there. Inoculation against disease is clearly no part of the educational responsibility of the school, nor does it further the school's educational function. The problem begins, however, when one tries to extend the child-benefit theory into such areas as publicly financed textbooks, teachers, library facilities, remedial reading programs, cultural enrichment couress, and the like. This is what Mr. Himmelfarb urges, and what certain recent state and federal programs seem to authorize.

Yet even a cursory examination of these benefits demonstrates that they function only to contribute to the educational program provided by the parochial school. Few children will voluntarily purchase or borrow textbooks for private pleasure. The textbook is thrust upon the child because the school administrator deems it a satisfactory instrument to further the total educational program and policy of the school. The same is true of all of the other categories of aid which I have enumerated: each one is solicited solely because the sectarian administrator of the school finds it suitable for achieving his primary purpose. The constitutional status of the child-benefit theory is only slightly higher than that of the Southern "interposition" theory, which would allow the state to place itself between the citizenry and the requirements of the federal Constitution. Interposition has been wholly discredited for over a century. It is likely that the child-benefit theory, with its backdoor applications, will earn the same fate. Indeed, in August, 1966, a New York Supreme Court judge dismissed this theory as being without merit.

Finally, there is an aspect of the church–state relationship which, although previously insignificant, has lately begun to assume larger proportions. I refer to the manner in which churches disrupt national and local policies of racial integration. In the large cities in particular, the parochial school is rapidly becoming the last haven of the segregationist. Just when efforts are being made to integrate the public school, at considerable stress and expense, parochial schools are claiming a share of public funds to develop and further their own ends. Naturally, the parochial-school cause has been strongly supported by segregationists. The assistance offered by racists may in many cases be unwelcome to the parochial school, but the fact remains that a system of parochial schools supported by public funds would eventually spell the death of integrated public schools, and indeed of public-school education in general. This is not conjecture. It is already happening in several urban areas.

We now face a most important decision in the matter of giving public aid to parochial schools and other church-controlled institutions. We must decide whether we will maintain our commitment to a secular government which will continue to provide the benefits of education and welfare to all citizens without regard to their color, their theological views, or their economic status, or whether we will support divisive, frequently undemocratic special-interest groups, and leave to them the task of performing major functions of our society and determining the course of our development. If we choose the latter course, either the state will ultimately destroy the existing freedom of the churches, or particular churches will ultimately control our government. No middle ground will be possible. No matter which one wins control, it is certain that individual freedom will be destroyed.

History has shown that the slightest breaks in the wall between church and state are likely to widen beyond repair. The deluge which follows can destroy the very values which our society is attempting to construct for itself. The only way this country can preserve its commitment to freedom, to racial equality, to non-sectarian public education, and to religious liberty, is to strengthen its commitment to the principle of absolute separation.

MILTON HIMMELFARB:

Let us ignore what Mr. Shapiro says I said. What does he say for himself?

Separation, for him, forbids government to "support, through the use of public money . . . any church, or all churches. . . ." Indirect support is forbidden, too, because "every church dollar saved from buying [secular] books or equipment or paying a [secular] teacher's salary can be used to further the school's purely religious aims." Surely he knows that a church school saves many dollars by being allowed to use governmental police, fire, and sanitation services. He must believe, then, that the school should either be taxed or be made to use commercial services (though I have never heard of a commercial fire department). The same logic would apply to a church-related family service or recreation facility. Above all, it would apply to the deductibility provisions in the federal and state income-tax codes—Mr. Shapiro did not need me to remind him of that. There are few churches or synagogues or seminaries that do not depend on their contributors' being allowed to claim a tax deduction. He must also say, therefore, that our income-tax laws are unconstitutional. What does *he* think would happen if the Supreme Court upheld his logic? *I* think that in no time at all the Constitution would be amended explicitly enough to make his kind of separationism as dead as chattel slavery.

Mr. Shapiro likes Professor LaNoue's argument against aid to non-public schools, that because "no taxpayer has a legal right to send his child to a particular parochial school nor to vote for the persons who decide [its] educational policies," therefore "public aid to parochial schools necessarily forces *every* taxpayer to support two school systems, one of which represents and exists for the benefit of only a portion of the community." To see how good this argument is, for "parochial school" let us substitute "M.I.T." Then, if we accept the Shapiro–LaNoue reasoning, we must conclude that municipal services and tax-deductible contributions for M.I.T. are unconstitutional.

No taxpayer has a legal right to send his child to M.I.T. or to elect its trustees, and it represents only a portion of the community —a small one, the intellectually gifted and scientifically inclined. Since the power to tax is the power to destroy, Shapiro and LaNoue would just about outlaw any educational institution not run by a government, from a kindergarten to an institute of advanced study. They might even be outlawing state universities: no taxpayer has a legal right to send his child to most state universities (or their more respected divisions) if the child is not bright.

Mr. Shapiro and Professor LaNoue deny that parochial schools are for the benefit of the whole community. (Some—the anti-technologists—might deny that M.I.T. is beneficial; others might deny that the Guggenheim Museum is; but let that pass.) There are several reasons for asserting that parochial schools do benefit the whole community. One is this: the researchers have found—often disapprovingly, because they would like the graduates of parochial schools to be a little different—that parochial schools educate students who become citizens with about the same civic attitudes and behavior as most other Americans.

He is, Mr. Shapiro tells us, a disciple of eighteenth-century rationalism, or the Enlightenment. That he is—but not, I fear, of the Enlightenment at its best. His is an archaic doctrine of individualism, which sees either discrete individuals or the society–state with nothing mediating or intervening between the two. When it does see an association that encompasses less than society as a whole, it becomes indignant. After the Revolution had abolished the guilds and the estates, the French declared the early trade unions to be illegal conspiracies; and the same kind of individualist doctrine or ideology led to the same result, at about the same time, in the United States. I am not saying that Mr. Shapiro is against unions—that is not the normal flaw of eighteenth-century rationalists in the twentieth century. I am saying he has still to learn that individuals can differ from each other in outlooks arising from distinctive traditions and identifications; and that these, so far from stifling individuality, may actually nourish much of what people consider most worthy and individual in themselves.

Why is Mr. Shapiro's libertarian separationism especially common among Jews of the same kind as he? He deals with that question by obtuse denial. His views, he says, were not part of his heredity. Which is to say, being a Jew is not much more than a biological datum. But if this obtuseness is uncharacteristic of Mr. Shapiro from one point of view, from another it is entirely characteristic of the group to which he belongs—without his wanting to recognize that he belongs to it.

By an individual pursuit of universal reason, Mr. Shapiro thinks, he has arrived at his beliefs and conclusions. So think other Jews like him. They are a regiment of individualists marching in step, each assuming that the rhythm is his own. Granted that it is universal reason which beats the drum, why is the beat heard with such disproportionate acuity by people of a certain kind? Especially must we ask this since they do not understand that to others they appear as only one group of marchers among many, every one with its distinctive manner and banner, and not a few with conflicting pretensions to universalism.

In the June, 1961 *Commentary,* Daniel P. Moynihan wrote about Reform and regular Democrats. The Reformers, he said, were liberals, mostly Jews. They were incapable of conceding legitimacy to others' habits of thought, or putting themselves in others' shoes, or realizing that in the others' eyes they were a cohesive self-interest bloc—for instance, the speaker at a conference on legislative issues in New York who

> warned that a higher-education bond issue . . . would permit building loans to *parochial* colleges. The regulars react to this much as the liberals would react to a speech by a Bronx Italian protesting that an increase in competitive state scholarships for higher education would only give further advantage to the children of middle-class Jews—a view not unknown in Albany, but emphatically not expressed.

Mr. Shapiro defends "the right to express unpopular thoughts . . . without being punished." He hardly means the right to express thoughts about electronic music. He means someone's right to say he is not a Christian, or a believer in any religion for that matter. Since everyone has that right, the crucial word must be "punished." If you are in a minority, you are apt to be unpopular—that is almost a tautology. Mr. Shapiro wants to be popular while being in the minority. Otherwise, he feels, he is being punished.

Let us talk about Jews again. Remove Christian religious influence from the public schools as completely as you wish, you are not going to change the fact that in the best circumstances a Jew is sometimes going to feel like an outsider—and therefore, in Mr. Shapiro's view, punished—in an English-language culture of Chaucer and Shakespeare and T. S. Eliot and Ezra Pound, of Milton and Hawthorne. Or take culture in the anthropologist's sense. Having removed Christmas from the schools, if that were fully possible, you couldn't remove it from the street or the stores or television. The message of American culture to a Jewish child is, Yes, Ruthie, there is a Santa Claus; and No, he isn't Jewish.

If you think of our minority status as punishment, you will naturally want to escape it. What can help? The Revolution? No; witness Russia. The conversion of multitudes to Judaism? For that you may have to await the Messiah. Going to Israel? That would work. But here in America, the only thing that can help and is in your power to do, is to go over to the majority, to become or pretend to become a Christian; then at least your grandchildren will not feel punished. That is what is implied in equating minority status with punishment.

On the other hand, you would see unpopularity—which nowadays is less than it used to be, anyway—as a price, and minority status as the good for which you pay the price; and well worth it. Moderns don't like to be caught quoting the *Rubaiyat*, but most of us remember those verses: "I wonder often what the vintners buy/One-half so precious as the stuff they sell." What is a possible Jewish symbolism here? The vintners are some Jews; the wine they are eager to rid themselves of is Judaism, or the state or quality of being a Jew; what they buy is something they regard as more valuable, freedom from a minority condition experienced as punishment; but the poet knows they are getting the worse of the bargain.

Have I built too much on Mr. Shapiro's "punishment"? I hope that this isn't really what he meant.

Mr. Shapiro declares himself against a state of affairs in which particular theological attitudes are supported by public officials— a bold declaration, which will earn him the hostility of one in a thousand. If he thinks he is talking about something in the last third of the twentieth century and not in the eighteenth, that can only be because he has his own notions of theological attitudes. He can't reconcile himself to the tangle of religion and society. The prohibition of polygamy having been largely Christian in origin, Mr. Shapiro could say that the states and the federal government have no right to legislate that prohibition. (I would not be upset if polygamy were allowed to the schismatic Mormons still practicing it in the wilds of Arizona, and being jailed for it.) Or Mr. Shapiro could agree with Timothy Leary that it is a religious (Christian or Judeo-Christian) abuse of the power of the state which prevents him from propagating cultic marijuana and LSD. Or again, the next generation of high-school rebels, after the current Beatle-browed boys, may be nudists. Mr. Shapiro would then argue, I imagine, that a principal who forbade their coming naked to class was an official with a particular theological attitude, enforcing theological doctrines—residual Puritanism probably.

If Mr. Shapiro does not take all these positions, then let him stop talking so grandly and abstractly about non-believers being punished and the freedom of society being diminished. If he wants to talk about censorship, fine; but he should really not try to suggest that it typically arises because some clergyman may deem a film hostile to his group. The more likely situation, here and now, is that some civil-rights leader may deem something hostile to *his* group —like *Birth of a Nation,* or that mural in a Long Island bank with Banjo Billy in it. Mr. Shapiro's clergyman is pretty much a red herring, unless the reference is to Dr. King. But Dr. King is a race leader, too.

An exercise for separationists: separate church and state in Dr. King.

"The parochial-school issue," says Mr. Shapiro, "is purely and simply a question of money, as far as the advocates of public aid are concerned." Well, questions of money are not all that ignoble: in my public school, I was taught that on account of taxes the English gloriously beheaded a king and the American colonies declared their independence. And what's in it for Walter Lippmann and the *New Republic,* both of whom support federal aid to parochial schools?

Mr. Shapiro goes on to say that the Catholics' "standing as Americans is not in question, and undoubtedly is not felt by them to be an issue." Undoubtedly. Mr. Johnson, a President, can feel hurt by the disdain of the intellectuals and academics, but Mr. Shapiro knows that Catholics don't feel hurt by the disdain of a related group, those who call themselves libertarian separationists. Does he think Catholics don't overhear what libertarian separationists say to each other "in many Eastern suburbs when school-bond issues are voted upon"? He ought to read that article by Moynihan.

I marvel at the Catholics' forbearance. Mr. Shapiro is not alone in being "practical" and complaining that Catholics are getting $15 million of New York State's $65 million of federal funds for books and the like. The Catholic schools are enriching themseves at the expense of the public schools, he says. I fail to understand why to such accusations the Church doesn't give this answer: "Very well. We will stop. We will discontinue our parochial schools immediately and send our students to the public schools. Take back the $15 million." How much more than $15 million it would cost New York State in schools and teachers for those additional students, I don't know, but it might come to a billion or two. Then we would hear an outcry over school taxes that would make the present outcry over Catholic fiscal aggression sound like a lullaby. Some who now complain of the parochial schools would then be heard pleading with the Catholics to reconsider, and offering them rather more than $15 million to open their schools again. That "purely and simply a question of money" cuts both ways. We won't acknowledge that the Catholic schools save us a great deal more money than we accuse them of filching from us.

Anyway, Mr. Shapiro says, the parochial school isn't nice: "In the large cities in particular, the parochial school is rapidly becoming the last haven of the segregationist." But the parochial-school system is a century old, the Supreme Court's ruling against segregation is only twelve years old, and the parochial-school system still educates the same fraction of Catholic children of school age—half. The statistics reveal no irruption of segregationists in search of a haven.

Are the parochial schools of New Orleans a haven for segregationists? They had real integration before the public schools had token integration; and Leander Perez was excommunicated. I do not say it of Mr. Shapiro, but I have the impression that there are some who almost welcome the integration crisis in the public schools, as an occasion for putting the parochial schools in the wrong. What will they do when integration recedes as an issue?

"Attendance at a parochial school," Mr. Shapiro tells us, "is a matter of private choice, no different legally from giving a child private music lessons, or sending him to summer camp." And he is supposed to be replying to me. People who say that sort of thing hold parochial education to be private education, I wrote, and private education to be a luxury for the rich, like a Cadillac. Mr. Shapiro's Cadillac is summer camp and music lessons. So he couldn't have read what I wrote; or he couldn't have let it register.

Mr. Shapiro is engaging in selective perception, tuning out a message that makes him uncomfortable. His individualism blinds him to the reality of class—i.e., money, of all things: ". . . private choice . . . private music lessons. . . ." I wrote that the average Catholic has less money than the average Episcopalian, Congregationalist, or Jew, but that doesn't seem to have registered either. Apparently, Mr. Shapiro thinks most parents of parochial-school children can afford private music lessons and summer camp. (The going rate in the camps his friends send their children to is about a thousand dollars per child per summer.) Like much eighteenth-century individualism when it survives into the twentieth, Mr. Shapiro's is too formalist for substantive justice. If you can't afford your schools, he tells Catholic parents, that's not my problem; I have no obligation to indulge you in your taste for private luxuries.

For Mr. Shapiro, non-public education is something of a vice when too accessible for the common people. It can't quite be declared illegal, but sound public policy requires that we shall limit it to their betters by making it expensive. Equal justice, above all: non-public = non-public: parochial school = private school. We give no aid to the stockbroker with a child in a private school, we give no aid to the workman with children in a parochial school. Thus is justice not only done, but manifestly seen to be done.

The name of this philosophy is libertarian separationism.

Mr. Shapiro adds nothing to our understanding of the easy victory of our passion for separation over our compassion for the poor and our rationalization—"Blackmail!"—of our growing estrangement from a social liberalism that is prepared to compromise on church–state problems or bypass them. He doesn't deny that our emotion goes to separationism rather than to the poor. For myself, I wouldn't mind so much if at least we were torn. It is the ease even more than the fact of our separationism's victory that I object to.

A man I have known and respected for a long time has written me:

> I was a member of the [appropriate] committee of [an important Jewish organization]. It was an interesting experience. One of the most extraordinary happenings was the debate on the poverty and education bills. The passion with which the Wall was upheld would have been unbelievable to me if I had not been present. [X] made an appeal as vehement as if he were admonishing us to fight Hitler or Stalin. Dean Keppel, then the U.S. Commissioner of

Education, was received at the luncheon meeting at which he was guest of honor with such cool, formal courtesy and was asked such hostile questions that I was ashamed of myself for being present.

Passions spin the plot.

In his peroration, Mr. Shapiro is angry with "divisive, frequently undemocratic special-interest groups." That is strange language for a liberal. It is intolerant, authoritarian; it is how the Know-Nothings and the American Protective Association spoke of those sinister Catholics in the nineteenth centry, it is how some people speak of the Negroes now.

If we "leave to [those groups] the task of performing major functions of our society," Mr. Shapiro warns, "particular churches will ultimately control our government." My flesh is supposed to creep, but somehow it won't. What are the threats that serious people talk about? The threats of big government, big business, big labor, big communications, more recently big science, even big education. For the damage from all those bignesses, pluralism is, if not a preventive, at any rate a mitigative. Mr. Shapiro has earlier spoken of the widespread popular demand for a secularized society. How then can he tell us we are threatened by big religion, or big particular churches? (Of course he really means that big particular church.) I can understand why fearless spirits engaged in a critique of pure tolerance should be scornful of the tradition of liberal democracy, and therefore of its corollary, pluralism. What I can't understand is why a liberal democrat should be scornful of pluralism.

Last, and most solemnly: "History has shown that the slightest breaks in the wall between church and state are likely to widen beyond repar." (Or, as I quoted this dogma, in its more definitive formulation: "Religious freedom is most secure where church and state are separated, and least secure where church and state are united.") In one sentence Mr. Shapiro achieves two things. First he demonstrates again that he refuses to take in what he reads. I recalled some obvious facts disproving that statement—not proving its converse, just disproving it. Mr. Shapiro will not let so majestic an idea be undermined by paltry facts, so his eyes read but his mind remains closed.

Next he demonstrates that an asserted universalism can be quite provincial and particular. "History has shown...." History? Not Scandinavian or British history. At most, American history; and then very approximately, when seen by eyes eager to see. One tendentious concept of America is inflated and becomes universal humanity, always and everywhere. This is only ideology. We live in a room with a view, and think we behold the world under the aspect of eternity.

Now briefly to the letters published in October, or to those parts of them not answered in my answer to Mr. Shapiro. Like him, most of the writers of those letters are fundamentalists, repeating their creed. Hard as it may be for them to understand, I do not reject that creed out of ignorance. I am familiar with it, and I find it wanting.

Marcus Cohn: Since the watchword seems to be contemporary need, let us change our interpretation of the First Amendment to accord with contemporary need. We wouldn't leave it to the public to judge whether a licensee programs enough education or discussion, because we know how little the public is to be relied on for that sort of thing. When we're in earnest about something in radio or TV, we don't leave it to the public, we call for the FCC.

Lawrence K. Karlton: Libertarian separationists have been proclaiming, as if it were one of those self-evident truths, that "religious freedom is most secure where church and state are separated," etc. All I did was to remind us that that truth is false. Now, by some sleight of hand, the burden is put on me and I am asked to defend a ludicrous proposition I explicitly ruled out—that an arrangement suitable to Scandinavia must also be suitable to America.

Alexander Firestone: I did not say or imply that "any education reduces anti-Semitism" anywhere, especially in Germany one and two generations ago. I said, carefully: "All the evidence in America points to education, more than anything else, influencing adherence to democracy and egalitarianism. All the evidence points to Catholic parochial education having the same influence."

Gerson Jacobs: There is nothing sacred about "locally elected school boards"; Francis Keppel's *Necessary Revolution in American Education* has no high opinion of them. Non-public schools must meet the standards of state boards of education.

Ernest Alexander: To make religion or religious education responsible for French Canadian nationalism is a joke. French-speaking atheists in Quebec (there are some) can resent the English ascendancy as much as any believer. As for Holland and its "columnization"—which came first, Protestants and Catholics studying in their separate schools or a we–they tradition so old and so deep that Protestants and Catholics also shop in their separate department stores? The Spanish marriage was not the only one that failed to rejoice the Dutch. There was a German marriage, too. And we ought to remember not only the Dutch history of a long struggle for independence from Spain—the Inquisition, the Duke of Alva, and all that —but also the present reality of Franco and his kind of government.

David F. Greenberg: The government in effect pays part of the money I give to my synagogue, UJA, the Association on American Indian Affairs, Spanish Refugee Aid, the American Academy for Jewish Research, and the alumni association of my college, but I don't see the government controlling any of them. In general, I prefer indirect to direct support.

If I had mentioned Israel at all, it would have been as a particularly instructive example of how hard it is to erect a wall when state, society, nationality, culture, and religion are so entangled with each other. My opinions about religion in Israel are on record, in back issues.

Finally, John M. Kaufman: To be called disturbing is historically such an honor, however the epithet may be intended here, that I must reply, *Qatonti*, I am unworthy. Ahab thought Elijah disturbing: "Is it you, you troubler of Israel?"

I did *not* "attempt to link those who opposed the aid-to-education bill because of church–state objections with reactionaries and racists." I said of "the radical separationists" that "theirs is a true and not a feigned indignation," distinguishing them in that respect from the reactionary and racist opposition to the bill. And I find it particularly unfair of Mr. Kaufman to find unfair of me my citation of Theodore Leskes. I said that Leskes "was rather more convinced than I for the need for a wall." Of Leskes on the military chaplaincy, I said that "he could not object in principle," not that he had no objections to actual practice.

We must thank Mr. Kaufman for a remarkable theorem, that religious freedom in Great Britain is insecure, as well as for a highly original proof: the "quite shocking" difficulty in which Jewish children find themselves if they want to get into '"good"' schools. His own quotation marks tell us he isn't talking about good state schools, or even schools like Manchester Grammar, which technically qualifies as what the English call a public school; he is talking about schools like Eton and Harrow. He means there are Jews who are denied a good old-school tie, not a good education. That is to say, he is talking of social discrimination. The reason why there is social discrimination against English Jews he says, is that England has no separation of church and state. He must be right, because the United States has separation of church and state and American Jews have therefore never been kept out of neighborhoods, clubs, hotels, prep schools, colleges, or fraternities.

"Perhaps," he says, I am "not as concerned about the preservation of Judaism as the rest of us." From Mr. Kaufman's heartbreaking stories about glee clubs and Christmas plays I infer that he is partial to a punishment theory much like Mr. Shapiro's. Anyone who believes the grotesque proposition that a glee club's songs (carols?) lead to conversion, or who takes at face value a convert's statement that these caused his conversion, or who immortalizes in writing the fantasy that "this pattern [of conversion] is country-wide"—such a person, besides being awesomely credulous, is so palpably without a clue to Judaism that I am not overwhelmed by his concern for it. A Jewish attachment that could be killed by a carol wouldn't be weak, it would be dead to begin with. If Sandy Koufax can ask to be excused from pitching on Yom Kippur, a Jewish student can refrain from Christian carols.

Mr. Kaufman, so ready to believe the unbelievable, is unready to believe my quotation from a dead colleague. Nevertheless, I shall try again. Another colleague now dead was the social scientist Samuel H. Flowerman. I have forgotten what the occasion was—a discussion either of the tape recording Mr. Kaufman mentions or of the related, standard argument against released–dismissed time. The argument goes that released or dismissed time, by making children aware of religious differences, is divisive and produces discomfort in Jewish children. Flowerman said—and this is probably written down somewhere in some learned journal—that the facts alleged are not facts at all: it is an illusion of the *Konfessionslos* that a child is unaware of religious differences if his teacher doesn't bring them out. The child is not initially uncomfortable, Flowerman said, but uncomfortable parents project their own discomfort onto him, and later still he may catch it from them. The pathology is less in the situation and the child than in the parents.

The defense Mr. Kaufman offers us is worse than no defense at all. He wants us to kid ourselves. He would have us believe that we are not inherently and necessarily a minority, or that removing Christmas carols from the public schools is the same as removing the Christian foundation stones and building blocks of Western culture. I think that not Christmas carols but whining exaggerations of how hard it is to be a Jew turn young people away, and I think most young Jews know that it is easier to be a Jew today than it used to be. Better still, they enact that knowledge by being the kind of people they are. They seem to me in many ways less flawed than their parents' generation.

Let me ask the *ad hominem* critics of my position an *ab homine* question. You think you are better friends than I to the public schools and integration. You think I have a greater personal interest than you in aid to the non-public schools. Would you be willing to put that to the test of how many children you and I have in integrated public schools?

Chapter Four

Morality as Public Policy

Allied to the issue of church–state separation is the major question of how far the government may go in enforcing common standards of morality. While this problem generates intense feeling among religious groups especially, it is also a volatile subject with the general citizenry. The constitutionality of "censorship" or the enforcement of "public decency" does not center around the religion clause of the First Amendment, but it does fall under the guarantee of freedom of speech, which has gradually been extended to various forms of expression. The *Burstyn* v. *Wilson* decision of the Supreme Court is presented in this chapter in order to state cogently the issue of whether "sacrilege" is a crime punishable by governmental authority.

The question that the Supreme Court did not deal with, and has yet to define satisfactorily, is to what degree and upon what bases can freedom of expression be denied in the cause of public morals. In this area more than in nearly any other, court and public officials at all levels are constantly being pressured to protect the public standards of "decency" at the expense of individual expression and communication. Perhaps the First Amendment was badly phrased: a great deal of conflict might have been avoided by guaranteeing not the right of individual free expression, but rather the public's inalienable right to hear and see all modes of expression and all points of view. But as it stands, the courts must struggle to find expedient ways to protect the public's sensibilities as well as individuals' freedom of speech.

The problem of the relation between public policy and ethical–moral standards extends far beyond the domestic scene. Increasingly since World War II, through the Korean and Vietnamese conflicts, greater numbers of both intellectuals and the general public have questioned the morality of war and the ethical roots of our own foreign policy. International law and morality have been cited as bases for protests against United States policy in such areas as Vietnam, Cuba, and the Middle East. On the other hand those who have raised such objections have also been vociferous in their criticism of the moralistic foreign policies of men like John Foster Dulles.

The issue before the nation now is how the United States, the leading world power, can defend and promote its national interest (however defined) while providing a moral, ethical, and mature example of responsible leadership to other peoples. Perhaps another way to phrase it would be: Now that we have power, and the consequent prestige, what do we intend to do with it? The final selection in the book deals with this pressing concern.

Burstyn v. Wilson (1952)*

Appeal from the Court of Appeals of New York [to the United States Supreme Court].

MR. JUSTICE CLARK delivered the opinion of the Court.

The issue here is the constitutionality, under the First and Fourteenth Amendments, of a New York statute which permits the banning of motion picture films on the ground that they are "sacrilegious." That statute makes it unlawful

to exhibit, or to sell, lease or lend for exhibition at any place of amusement for pay or in connection with any business in the state of New York, any motion picture film or reel [with specified exceptions not relevant here], unless there is at the time in full force and effect a valid license or permit therefor of the education department....

The statute further provides:

The director of the [motion picture] division [of the education department] or, when authorized by the regents, the officers of a local office or bureau shall cause to be promptly examined every motion picture film submitted to them as herein required, and unless such film or a part thereof is obscene, indecent, immoral, inhuman, sacrilegious, or is of such a character that its exhibition would tend to corrupt morals or incite to crime, shall issue a license therefor. If such director, or, when so authorized, such officer shall not license any film submitted, he shall furnish to the applicant therefor a written report of the reasons for his refusal and a description of each rejected part of a film not rejected in toto.

---

* 343 U.S. 495, 96 L. Ed. 1098, 72 S. Ct. 777.

Appellant is a corporation engaged in the business of distributing motion pictures. It owns the exclusive rights to distribute throughout the United States a film produced in Italy entitled *The Miracle*. On November 30, 1950, after having examined the picture, the motion picture division of the New York education department, acting under the statute quoted above, issued to appellant a license authorizing exhibition of *The Miracle*, with English subtitles, as one part of a trilogy called *Ways of Love*. Thereafter, for a period of approximately eight weeks, *Ways of Love* was exhibited publicly in a motion picture theater in New York City under an agreement between appellant and the owner of the theater whereby appellant received a stated percentage of the admission price.

During this period, the New York State Board of Regents, which by statute is made the head of the education department, received "hundreds of letters, telegrams, post cards, affidavits and other communications" both protesting against and defending the public exhibition of *The Miracle*. The Chancellor of the Board of Regents requested three members of the Board to view the picture and to make a report to the entire Board. After viewing the film, this committee reported to the Board that in its opinion there was basis for the claim that the picture was "sacrilegious." Thereafter, on January 19, 1951, the Regents directed appellant to show cause, at a hearing to be held on January 30, why its license to show *The Miracle* should not be rescinded on that ground. Appellant appeared at this hearing, which was conducted by the same three-member committee of the Regents which had previously viewed the picture, and challenged the jurisdiction of the committee and of the Regents to proceed with the case. With the consent of the committee, various interested persons and organizations submitted to it briefs and exhibits bearing upon the merits of the picture and upon the constitutional and statutory questions involved. On February 16, 1951, the Regents, after viewing *The Miracle*, determined that it was "sacrilegious" and for that reason ordered the Commissioner of Education to rescind appellant's license to exhibit the picture. The Commissioner did so.

Appellant brought the present action in the New York courts to review the determination of the Regents. Among the claims advanced by appellant were (1) that the statute violates the Fourteenth Amendment as a prior restraint upon freedom of speech and of the press; (2) that it is invalid under the same Amendment as a violation of the guaranty of separate church and state and as a prohibition of the free exercise of religion; and, (3) that the term "sacrilegious" is so vague and indefinite as to offend due process. The Appellate Division rejected all of appellant's contentions and upheld the Regents' determination. 278 App.Div. 253, 104 N.Y.S.2d 740. On appeal the New York Court of Appeals, two judges dissenting, affirmed the order of the Appellate Division. 303 N.Y. 242, 101 N.E.2d. The case is here on appeal. 28 U.S.C. § 1257(2).

As we view the case, we need consider only appellant's contention that the New York statute is an unconstitutional abridgment of free speech and a free press. In *Mutual Film Corp.* v. *Industrial Comm'n.*, 236 U.S. 230 (1915), a distributor of motion pictures sought to enjoin the enforcement of an Ohio statute which required the prior approval of a board of censors before any motion picture could be publicly exhibited in the state, and which directed the board to approve only such films as it adjudged to be "of a moral, educational or amusing and harmless character." The statute was assailed in part as an unconstitutional abridgment of the freedom of the press guaranteed by the First and Fourteenth Amendments. The District Court rejected this contention, stating that the first eight Amendments were not a restriction on state action. 215 F. 138, 141 (D.C.N.D.Ohio 1914). On appeal to this Court, plaintiff in its brief abandoned this claim and contended merely that the statute in question violated the freedom of speech and publication guaranteed by the Constitution of Ohio. In affirming the decree of the District Court denying injunctive relief, this Court stated:

> It cannot be put out of view that the exhibition of moving pictures is a business pure and simple, originated and conducted for profit, like other spectacles, not to be regarded, nor intended to be regarded by the Ohio constitution, we think, as part of the press of the country or as organs of public opinion.

In a series of decisions beginning with *Gitlow* v. *New York*, 268 U.S. 652 (1925), this Court held that the liberty of speech and of the press which the First Amendment guarantees against abridgment by the federal government is within the liberty safeguarded by the Due Process Clause of the Fourteenth Amendment from invasion by state action. That principle has been followed and reaffirmed to the present day. Since this series of decisions came after the Mutual decision, the present case is the first to present squarely to us the question whether motion pictures are within the ambit of protection which the First Amendment, through the Fourteenth, secures to any form of "speech" or "the press."

It cannot be doubted that motion pictures are a significant medium for the communication of ideas. They may affect public attitudes and behavior in a variety of ways, ranging from direct espousal of a political or social doctrine to the subtle shaping of thought which characterizes all artistic expression. The importance of motion pictures as an organ of public opinion is not lessened by the fact that they are designed to entertain as well as to inform. . . .

It is urged that motion pictures do not fall within the First Amendment's aegis because their production, distribution, and exhibition is a large-scale business conducted for private profit. We cannot agree. That books, newspapers, and magazines are published and sold for profit does not prevent them from being a form of expression whose liberty is safeguarded by the First Amendment. We fail to see why operation for profit should have any different effect in the case of motion pictures.

It is further urged that motion pictures possess a greater capacity for evil, particularly among the youth of a community, than other modes of expression. Even if one were to accept this hypothesis, it does not follow that motion pictures should be disqualified from First Amendment protection. If there be capacity for evil it may be relevant in determining the permissible scope of community control, but it does not authorize substantially unbridled censorship such as we have here.

For the foregoing reasons, we conclude that expression by means of motion pictures is included within the free speech and free press guaranty of the First and Fourteenth Amendments. To the extent that language in the opinion in *Mutual Film Corp.* v. *Industrial Comm'n., supra,* is out of harmony with the views here set forth, we no longer adhere to it.[1]

To hold that liberty of expression by means of motion pictures is guaranteed by the First and Fourteenth Amendments, however, is not the end of our problem. It does not follow that the Constitution requires absolute freedom to exhibit every motion picture of every kind at all times and all places. That much is evident from the series of decisions of this Court with respect to other media of communication of ideas. Nor does it follow that motion pictures are necessarily

---

[1] See *United States* v. *Paramount Pictures, Inc.,* 334 U.S. 131, 166 (1948): "We have no doubt that moving pictures, like newspapers and radio, are included in the press whose freedom is guaranteed by the First Amendment." It is not without significance that talking pictures were first produced in 1926, eleven years after the Mutual decision. Encylopaedia Britannica (1951), "Motion Pictures." [Footnote by the Court.]

subject to the precise rules governing any other particular method of expression. Each method tends to present its own peculiar problems. But the basic principles of freedom of speech and the press, like the First Amendment's command, do not vary. Those principles, as they have frequently been enunciated by this Court, make freedom of expression the rule. There is no justification in this case for making an exception to that rule.

The statute involved here does not seek to punish, as a past offense, speech or writing falling within the permissible scope of subsequent punishment. On the contrary, New York requires that permission to communicate ideas be obtained in advance from state officials who judge the content of the words and pictures sought to be communicated. This Court recognized many years ago that such a previous restraint is a form of infringement upon freedom of expression to be especially condemned. *Near* v. *Minnesota ex. rel. Olson,* 283 U.S. 697 (1931). The Court there recounted the history which indicates that a major purpose of the First Amendment guaranty of a free press was to prevent prior restraints upon publication, although it was carefully pointed out that the liberty of the press is not limited to that protection. It was further stated that "the protection even as to previous restraint is not absolutely unlimited. But the limitation has been recognized only in exceptional cases." *Idem,* at 716. In the light of the First Amendment's history and of the *Near* decision, the State has a heavy burden to demonstrate that the limitation challenged here presents such an exceptional case.

New York's highest court says there is "nothing mysterious" about the statutory provision applied in this case: "It is simply this: that no religion, as that word is understood by the ordinary, reasonable person, shall be treated with contempt, mockery, scorn and ridicule. . . ." This is far from the kind of narrow exception to freedom of expression which a state may carve out to satisfy the adverse demands of other interests of society. In seeking to apply the broad and all-inclusive definition of "sacrilegious" given by the New York courts, the censor is set adrift upon a boundless sea amid a myriad of conflicting currents of religious views, with no charts but those provided by the most vocal and powerful orthodoxies. New York cannot vest such unlimited restraining control over motion pictures in a censor. Cf. *Kunz* v. *New York,* 340 U.S. 290 (1951).

Since the term "sacrilegious" is the sole standard under attack here, it is not necessary for us to decide, for example, whether a state may censor motion pictures under a clearly-drawn statute designed and applied to prevent the showing of obscene films. That is a very different question from the one now before us. We hold only that under the First and Fourteenth Amendments a state may not ban a film on the basis of a censor's conclusion that it is "sacrilegious."

But is it Legal?*

Gore Vidal

In 1963, H. L. A. Hart, Oxford Professor of Jurisprudence, gave three lectures at Stanford University. In these lectures (now published as *Law, Liberty and Morality* [1]) Professor Hart attempted to answer the old question: Is the fact that certain conduct is by common standards immoral sufficient cause to punish that conduct by law? A question which leads him to what might be a paradox: "Is it morally permissible to enforce morality as such? Ought immorality as such to be a crime?" Philosophically, Professor Hart inclines to John Stuart Mill's celebrated negative. In the essay "On Liberty," Mill wrote, "The only purpose for which power can rightfully be exercised over any member of a civilized community against his will is to prevent harm to others"; and to forestall the arguments of the paternally minded, Mill added that a man's

> own good, either physical or moral, is not a sufficient warrant. He cannot rightfully be compelled to do or forbear because it will be better for him to do so, because it will make him happier, because in the opinions of others, to do so would be wise or even right.

Now it would seem that at this late date in the Anglo-American society, the question of morality and its relation to the law has been pretty much decided. In general practice, if not in particular statute, our society tends to keep a proper distance between the two. Yet national crisis may, on occasion, bring out the worst in our citizenry. In 1917 while our boys were over there, a working majority of the Congress decided that drink was not only sinful for the moral man but bad for the physical man. The result was Prohibition. After a dozen years of living with the Great Experiment, the electorate finally realized that moral legislation on such a scale is impossible to enforce. A lesson was learned and one would have thought it

---

* Reprinted from Gore Vidal, "But Is It Legal?", *Partisan Review*, XXXII (Winter, 1965), 79–87, by permission.
[1] (Stanford, Calif.: Stanford Univ. Press 1963).

unlikely that the forces which created the Volstead Act could ever again achieve a majority. But today odd things are happening in the Republic, as well as in the Kingdom across the water where Professor Hart detects a revival of what he calls "legal moralism," and he finds alarming certain recent developments.

In the days of the Star Chamber, to conspire to corrupt public morals was a common law offense. Needless to say, this vague catch-all turned out to be a marvelous instrument of tyranny and it was not entirely abandoned in England until the eighteenth century. Now it has been suddenly revived as a result of the 1961 case, *Shaw* v. *Director of Public Prosecutions*. Shaw was an enterprising pimp who published a magazine called *Ladies Directory*, which was just that. Despite this useful contribution to the gallantry of England, Shaw was found guilty of three offenses. Publishing an obscene article. Living on the earnings of prostitutes. Conspiring to corrupt public morals. The last offense delighted the legal moralists. There was much satisfied echoing of the eighteenth-century Lord Mansfield's statement, "Whatever is *contra bonos mores et decorum* the principles of our laws prohibit and the King's Court as the general censor and guardian of the public morals is bound to restrain and punish." As a result of the decision against Mr. Shaw, it is now possible to ban a book like *Lady Chatterley's Lover* on the imprecise grounds that it will corrupt public morals, and a lecture by Mr. Norman O. Brown could end in arrest. The possibilities for persecution in the name of public morals (themselves ill-defined) are endless and alarming. Though various American states still retain "conspiring to corrupt" statutes, they are largely cherished as relics of our legal origins in the theocratic code of Oliver Cromwell. The last serious invoking of this principle occurred in 1935 when the Nazis solemnly determined that anything was punishable if it was deserving of punishment according "to the fundamental conceptions of penal law and sound popular feeling."

Defining immorality is of course not an easy task, though English judges and American state legislatures seem not to mind taking it on. Lord Devlin, a leader of the legal moralists, has said "that the function of the criminal law is to enforce a moral principle and nothing else." How does Lord Devlin arrive at a moral principle? He appeals to the past. What is generally said to be wrong is wrong, while "a recognized morality is as necessary to society's existence as a recognized government." Good. But Lord Devlin does not acknowledge that there is always a considerable gap between what is officially recognized as good behavior and what is in actual fact countenanced and practiced. Though adultery in England is thought to be morally wrong, there are not statutes under which a man may be punished for sleeping with someone else's wife. Adultery is not a legal offense, nor does it presumably arouse in the public "intolerance, indignation, and disgust," the three emotions which Lord Devlin insist are inevitably evoked by those acts which offend the accepted morality. Whenever this triad is present, the law must punish. Yet how is one to measure "intolerance, indignation, and disgust"? Without an appeal to Dr. Gallup, it would be difficult to decide what, if anything, the general public really thinks about these matters. Without a referendum, it is anyone's guess to what degree promiscuity, say, arouses disgust in the public. Of course Lord Devlin is not really arguing for this sort of democracy. His sense of right and wrong is based on what he was brought up to believe was right and wrong, as prescribed by church and custom.

In the realm of sexual morals, all things take on a twilight shade. Off and on for centuries, homosexuality has aroused the triple demon in the eyes of many. But a majority? It would be surprising if it did, knowing what we now know about the extent—if not the quality— of human sexual behavior. In any case, why should homosexual acts between consenting adults be considered inimical to the public good? This sort of question raises much heat, and the invoking of "history." According to Lord Devlin, "the loosening of moral bonds is often the first stage of [national] disintegration." Is it? The periods in history which are most admired by legal moralists tend to be those vigorous warlike times when a nation is pursuing a successful and predatory course of military expansion, such as the adventures of Sparta, Alexander, Julius Caesar, Frederick of Prussia. Yet a reading of history ought to convince Lord Devlin that these militaristic societies were not only brutish and "immoral" by any standard but startlingly homosexual. What was morally desirable in a Spartan army officer is now punished in Leicester Square. Obviously public attitudes have changed since those vigorous days. Does that then mean that laws should alter as old prejudices are replaced by new? In response to public opinion, the Emperor Justinian made homosexuality a criminal offense on the grounds that buggery, as everyone knew, was the chief cause of earthquakes.

With the decline of Christianity in the last two centuries, the legal moralists have more and more used the state to punish sin. One of Lord Devlin's allies, J. G. Stephen, in "Liberty, Equality, Fraternity," comes straight to the point. Referring to moral offenders, he

writes, "The feeling of hatred and the desire of vengeance are important elements in human nature which ought, in such cases, to be
satisfied in a regular public and legal manner." There is the case not
only for capital punishment, but for public hangings all in the name
of the Old Testament God of vengeance. Or as Lord Goddard puts it,
"I do not see how it can be either non-Christian, or other than praise-
worthy, that the country should be willing to avenge crime." Yet
Stephen also realizes that for practical purposes "you cannot punish
anything which public opinion as expressed in the common practice
of society does not strenuously and unequivocally condemn. To be
able to punish, a moral majority must be overwhelming." But is there
such a thing as a moral majority in sexual matters? Professor Hart
thinks not.

> The fact that there is lip service to an official sexual morality should
> not lead us to neglect the possibility that in sexual, as other mat-
> ters, there may be a number of mutually tolerant moralities, and
> that even where there is some homogeneity of practice and belief,
> offenders may be viewed not with hatred or resentment, but with
> amused contempt or pity.

In the United States the laws determining correct human behavior are the work of the state legislatures. Over the years these
solemn assemblies have managed to make a complete hash out of
it, pleasing no one. The present tangled codes go back to the
founding of the country. When the Cromwells fell, the disgruntled
Puritans left England for Holland. To put it baldly, they departed
not because they were persecuted for their religious beliefs but
because they were forbidden to persecute others for *their* beliefs.
Holland took them in, and promptly turned them out. Only North
America was left. Here, as lords of the wilderness, they were free
to create the sort of quasi-theocratic society they had dreamed of.
Rigorously persecuting one another for religious heresies, witch-
craft, sexual misbehavior, they formed that ugly polity whose de-
cendants we are. As religious fundamentalists, they were irresistibly
drawn to the Old Testament God at his most forbidding and cruel,
while the sternness of St. Paul seemed to them far more agreeable
than the occasional charity of Jesus. Since adultery was forbidden
by the Seventh Commandment and fornication was condemned in
two of St. Paul's memos, the Puritans made adultery and fornication criminal offenses even though no such laws existed in England,
before or after Cromwell's reign. As new American states were
formed, they modeled their codes on those of the original states.

To this day, forty-three states will punish a single act of adulterous intercourse, while twenty-one states will punish fornication between unmarried people. In no other Western country is fornication a criminal offense. As for adultery, England, Japan and the Soviet Union have no such statutes; France and Italy will punish adultery under special conditions (e.g., if the man should establish the mistress in the family home); Germany and Switzerland punish adultery only if a court can prove that a marriage has been dissolved because of it.

In actual practice, the state laws are seldom invoked, although 242 Bostonians were arrested for adultery as recently as 1948. These statutes are considered "dead-letter laws" and there are those who argue that since they are so seldom invoked, why repeal them? One answer came in 1917 when a number of racketeers were arrested by the Federal government because they had taken girl friends to Florida, violating the Mann Act as well as the local fornication–adultery statutes. This case (*Caminetti* v. *United States*) set a dangerous precedent. Under a busy Attorney General, the "dead-letter laws" could be used to destroy all sorts of opponents, villainous or otherwise.

Rape is another offense much confused by state laws. During the thirties, out of 2366 New York City indictments, only 18 per cent were for forcible rape. The remaining 82 per cent were for statutory rape, a peculiar and imprecise crime. For instance, in Colorado it is statutory rape if intercourse takes place between an unmarried girl under eighteen and a man over eighteen. In practice this means that a boy of nineteen who has an affair with a consenting girl of seventeen is guilty of statutory rape. All the girl needs to do is to accuse her lover of consensual relations and he can be imprisoned for as long as fifty years. There are thousands of "rapists" serving time because, for one reason or another, they were found guilty of sexual intercourse with a willing partner.

In nearly every state fellatio, cunnilingus and anal intercourse are punished. Not only are these acts forbidden between men, they are forbidden between men and women, even within wedlock. As usual, the various state laws are in wild disarray. Ohio, the mother of Presidents, deplores fellatio but tolerates cunnilingus. In another state, sodomy is punished with a maximum twenty-year sentence, while fellatio calls for only three years, a curious discrimination. Deviate sexual acts between consenting adults are punished in most states, sentences running from three years to life imprisonment.

Of the other countries of the West, only England and Germany enter this area at all.

Elsewhere in the field of moral legislation, twenty-seven states forbid sexual relations and/or marriage between the white race and its inferiors: Negroes, American Indians, Orientals; and our narcotic laws are the scandal of the West. With the passage in 1914 of the Harrison Act, addiction to narcotics was found to be not the result of illness or bad luck, but of sin and sin must of course be punished by the state. For half a century the federal government has had a splendid time playing cops and robbers. And since you cannot have cops without robbers, they have created the robbers by maintaining that the sinful taking of drugs must be wiped out by law. As a result, the government's severity boosts the price of drugs, makes the game more desperate for addicts as well as pushers, encourages crime which in turn increases the payroll of the Narcotics Bureau. This lunatic state of affairs could exist only in a society still obsessed by the idea that the punishing of sin is the responsibility of the state. Yet in those countries where dope addiction is regarded as a matter for the doctor not the police, there can be no criminal traffic in drugs. In England there are 550 drug addicts. In New York City there are 23,000 addicts.

Theoretically the American separation of church and state should have left the individual's private life to his conscience. But this was not to be the case. The states promptly took it upon themselves to regulate the private lives of the citizens, flouting, many lawyers believe, the spirit if not the letter of the Constitution. The result of the experiment is all around us. One in eight Americans is mentally disturbed, and everywhere psychiatry flourishes. Our per capita acts of violence are beyond anything known to the other countries of the West, making our city streets unsafe for Peggy Goldwater and Mamie Eisenhower to walk. Clearly the unique attempt to make private morality answerable to law has not been a success. What to do?

On April 25, 1955, a committee of The American Law Institute presented a Model Penal Code (tentative draft number four) to the Institute which was founded some forty years ago "to promote the clarification and simplification of the law and its better adaptation to social needs." This Code represented an attempt to make sense out of conflicting laws, to remove "dead-letter laws" which might, under pressure, be reactivated or used for sinister ends, and to recognize that there is an area of private sexual morality which is no concern of the state. In this the Code echoed the recommendation of the Wolfenden Report which said: "Unless a deliberate attempt is to be made by society, acting through the agency of the law, to equate the sphere of crime with that of sin, there must remain a realm of private morality and immorality which is, in brief and crude terms, not the law's business."

The drafters of the Code proposed that adultery and sodomy between consenting adults be removed from the sphere of the law on the grounds that

> the Code does not attempt to use the power of the state to enforce purely moral or religious standards. We deem it inappropriate for the government to attempt to control behavior that has no substantial significance except as to the morality of the actor. Such matters are best left to religious, educational and other influences.

The Committee's recommendation on adultery was accepted. But there was a difference of opinion about sodomy. Judge John J. Parker spoke for the legal moralists:

> There are many things that are denounced by the criminal civil code in order that society may know that the state disapproves. When we fly in the face of public opinion, as evidenced by the code of every state in this union, we are not proposing a code which will commend itself to the thoughtful. . . .

Judge Parker was answered by Judge Learned Hand who said,

> Criminal law which is not enforced practically is much worse than if it was not on the books at all. I think homosexuality is a matter of morals, a matter very largely of taste, and it is not a matter that people should be put in prison about.

Judge Hand's position was upheld by the Institute.

As matters now stand only the state of Illinois has attempted to modify its sex laws. As of 1962, there is no longer any penalty in Illinois for the committing of a deviate sexual act. On the other hand an "open and notorious" adulterer can still be punished with a year in prison and fornication can be punished with six months in prison. So it is still taken for granted that the state has the right to regulate private behavior, in the interest of public morality.

One of the odd post-war phenomena has been the slowness of the liberal community to respond to those flaws in our society which might be corrected by concerted action. It is, of course, exhilarating to determine to what degree Hannah Arendt was responsible for Hitler. Yet it would seem to me that a change in the legal codes of the fifty American states might be almost as interesting an occupation for the liberally inclined as the fixing of past guilt and the analysis of old crimes. As they stand, the laws affect nearly everyone; implemented, they affect millions. Originally, the United States made a brave distinction between church and state. But then we put within the legal province of the states that which rightfully was religion's concern, and for those not susceptible to religious discipline, the concern of the moral conscience of the individual. The result has caused much suffering. The state laws are executed capriciously and though in time they may wither away, without some organized effort, they could continue for generations. In fact, there are signs today that the legal conservatives are at work strengthening these laws. In Florida the administration has distributed an astonishing pamphlet denouncing homosexuals in terms of seventeenth-century grandeur. In Dallas a stripper named Candy Barr was given an unprecedented fifteen-year prison term, ostensibly because she was found with marijuana in her possession, but actually because she was a sinful woman. In the words of a Dallas lawyer, the jury was "showing the world they were in favor of God, heaven, and sending to hell-fire a girl who violated their sense of morality."[2]

In this lowering Goldwater time, there is a strong movement afoot to save society from sexual permissiveness. Guardians of the oldtime virtue would maintain what they believe to be the status quo. They speak of "common decency" and "accepted opinion." But do such things really exist? And if they do, are they "right"? After all, there is no position so absurd that you cannot get a great many people to assume it. Lord Maugham, a former Lord Chancellor (where do they find them?), was convinced that the decline of the Roman Empire was the result of too frequent bathing. Justinian *knew* there was a causal link between buggery and earthquakes, while our great grandparents, as Steven Marcus recently reminded us, believed that masturbation caused insanity. I suspect that our own faith in psychiatry will seem as touchingly quaint to the future as our grandparents' belief in phrenology seems now to us. At any given moment, public opinion is a chaos of superstition, misinformation and prejudice. Even if one could accurately interpret it, would that be a reason for basing the law upon a consensus? Neither Professor Hart nor the legal moralists go that far. The conservatives are very much aware that they are living in an age of "moral decline." They wish to return to a stern morality like that of Cato

---

[2] Warren Leslie, *Dallas, Public and Private* (New York: Grossman Publishers).

or of Calvin. Failing that, they will settle for maintaining existing laws, the harsher the better. Professor Hart, on the other hand, believes that between what the law says people ought to do in their private lives and what they do, there is a considerable division. To the degree that such laws ought, ideally, to conform with human practice, he is a democrat. In answering those who feel that despite what people actually do, they ought not to do it, he remarks that this may be true, yet

> the use of legal punishment to freeze into immobility the morality dominant at a particular time in a society's existence may possibly succeed, but even where it does it contributes nothing to the survival of the animating spirit and formal values of social morality and may do much harm to them.

There is some evidence that by fits and starts the United States is achieving a civilization. Our record so far has not been distinguished, no doubt because we had a bad beginning. Yet it is always possible to make things better—as well as worse. Various groups are now at work trying to make sense of the fifty state codes. New York and California are expected to have improved codes by the end of this decade. But should there be a sudden renewal of legal moralism, attempts to modify and liberalize will fail. What is needed, specifically, is a test case before the Supreme Court which would establish in a single decision that "sin," where it does not disturb the public order, is not the concern of the state. This conception is implicit in our Constitution. But since it has never been tested, our laws continue to punish the sinful as though the state were still an arm of Church Militant. Although a Great Society is more easily attained in rhetoric than in fact, a good first step might be the removal from our statute books of that entirely misplaced scarlet letter.

Culture, Morals, and the Law*

One of the most challenging problems faced by clergy and concerned laymen of all religious persuasions is that of affecting the quality of modern life. In this time of cultural transition and value confusion, traditional religious

---

* From Chapter VI, "Cultural Freedom," and Chapter VII, "Morals and the Law," in *Religion and American Society*, by William Clancy, John Cogley, Arthur A. Cohen, Robert Gordis, William Gorman, S. Ernest Johnson, Robert Lekachman, and William Lee Miller; with an Introduction by Henry P. Van Dusen (Santa Barbara, California: Center for the Study of Democratic Institutions, 1961), pp. 62–72. Reprinted by permission.

tenets and standards of moral behavior have lost ground to expediency and "relativism." The following selection addresses itself to the necessity for the infusion of Christian principles into the secular culture by example and persuasion, rather than the negative suppression of ideas and practices through the support of coercive and restrictive laws.

Cultural Freedom

Though the church–state question is very important, not every significant controversy about religion and society is centered on that relationship. Some of our most abiding problems are concerned with the way church bodies attempt to exercise religious influence on the world of culture. Here, what strikes us as the great need is not so much knowledge of the law as a clearer understanding of what, in our discussions, we came to call the "canons of civic prudence." For, just as all that is desirable is not subject to legislation, so not all that is undesirable is illegal; a religious group might be acting quite within the law and still be worthy of censure.

What we are concerned with here, basically, is the question of how church bodies may bring the "truths" of their faith to bear on the secular culture.

One easy but unsatisfactory solution to the question is simply to deny the right of religious groups to apply their convictions to the life of society. Those who propose this solution seem to be demanding that religious concerns be shelved for six days a week in the interests of civic harmony. But the churches look upon this as too high a price to pay for civic harmony; moreover, many persons, including many outside the churches, would question the value of a "harmony" to be achieved by suppression of this sort.

At the opposite end there are church folk who seem to feel that because we Americans are a "religious people" religious values— or at least the values of the religious majority—should dominate cultural life.

We find neither of these positions acceptable. A concern for freedom prompts us to believe that religious citizens should not be required to bottle up their highest aspirations for the secular society; the same concern prompts us to insist that no one should be required against his will to behave as if he believed in this or that religious value merely because a dominant group has the power of numbers or of influence to enforce its standards on all.

Almost all religious communities claim to have a special grasp of theological truth. Of course some claims are more inclusive than others; some groups put more emphasis than others on their church's authority to interpret the law of God. The free society as such is neutral about all such claims. But so long as religious groups accept the basic charter of agreements that bind the American people into a civic unity, the nation has a right to expect religious groups, whatever their theological claims, not to impose their special "truths" on others, by social coercion, by the use of economic pressures, political threats, boycotts, or blacklists.

As Robert Lekachman wrote in *The Churches and the Public:* "The free society encourages the honorable expression of many beliefs. It is also a society in which the rules of the game are themselves a shared value." The "shared value" in question here might be put this way: Persuasion is the proper mode of action for American groups that would transform society; coercion, direct or indirect, or the suppression of ideas is properly held anathema.

Admittedly, persuasion is a long, painful process and not always successful. A picket-line outside a theatre or a skillful power-play in a local community — the "right" telephone call or the "word" passed along to a librarian, a bookstore salesman, or a theatre-owner — can often succeed in doing what the arts of oratory have failed to do; a political officeholder arbitrarily declaring a policy ban at the behest of one or another religious group, or a police chief finding a specious reason why a movie should not be shown, a lecture not given, or a book not sold, can accomplish in an hour what may take years to bring about by the conscientious use of pulpit or podium — the disappearance of a "bad" idea. But the religious group that respects the canons of civic prudence will not take these shortcuts to success.

There are both moral and pragmatic reasons why the shortcuts should be avoided. For one thing, they are rarely effective over the long haul. A nation converted against its will remains unconverted still. Moreover, in attempting to uphold one set of values— be it "decency," "tolerance," or "historical accuracy"—held by one group in society, they tear at the fabric of civic peace, which is a value necessary for the whole society.

We cannot say what evils were prevented by the use of pressure groups in successfully preventing movies from being shown, books from being sold, lectures from being given, or ideas from being expressed; nevertheless we seriously doubt that if they were balanced against the harm done to community relations by the ill-feeling and dissension caused by coercive activities of this kind, the evils avoided would be outweighed by the harm actually done.

Are we, then, saying that religious groups must be indifferent to what movies are shown, what books sold, what lectures given, what ideas expressed? No. We are saying that religious groups and their leaders have a right to preach against movies, books, lectures, and "bad" ideas, or even to proscribe them for their own members. They may do this by any means they choose, in accordance with their own rules—by publishing forbidden lists, attaching ecclesiastical penalties, even by threatening excommunication if that is their law.

Moreover, the efforts of religious leaders need not be confined to their own followers. A religious group, relying on the arts of publicity and persuasion, should be left free to form public opinion about movies, books, lectures, ideas. When they do so, they will be acting in accordance with the nation's best traditions. We are not arguing against activities of this sort. What we object to, rather, is the use of coercive measures that depend ultimately not on their appeal to the opinion of the public but on the use of the economic and political powers of sectarian groups.

As we have already said, such activities may be within the letter of the law; yet it seems to us that groups truly dedicated to the preservation of our society will not hesitate to abide by our unwritten laws; they will scrupulously observe respect for America's belief in the free flow of information and at least tolerate the expression of all ideas, good, bad, and indifferent.

In one way or another, all religious groups benefit from this American trait. For at least some of the ideas and practices of any one religious group are distasteful to some other group, yet all find it possible to carry on. For example, what appears to be solemn worship for one may be regarded as errant idolatry by another; what is believed to be a divinely authorized discipline by one may appear to be spiritual slavery to another; what is regarded as an expression of liberty of conscience to one may be abhorrent to another that sees in it only theological chaos. Despite potential dissensions, however, all these groups generally manage to live in peace with their rivals. They tolerate each other, even though they may regard each other's beliefs as intolerable. If you ask why, we will have to say that it is because they have learned to behave according to the demands of civility.

Protestants do not picket Roman Catholic churches, though there may be nothing illegal in their doing so. They are content, rather, to attend their own services. Catholics do not threaten to withhold business patronage from those who contribute to Protestant churches, though they might be able to do so without landing in jail. Jews and Christians of all persuasions have learned how to disagree on theological matters without breaking the bonds of civic friendship. So have Protestants and Catholics, even though Protestants are convinced Catholics are wrong in their interpretation of Christianity and Catholics are persuaded that Protestants are wrong in theirs. Moreover, if not directly at least by implication, Catholicism is preached against in Protestant churches, Protestantism is preached against in Catholic churches, and both forms of Christianity are preached against in Jewish pulpits.

The churches in their day-by-day relationships with each other, then, offer an example of how they themselves ought to act in regard to the secular culture. They are free to denounce it, to preach in favor of their own version of what it should be, to do all in their persuasive powers to get others to agree with them, and most of all to contribute to it. At the same time they must be content to suffer the cultural propagation of what they regard as "error"—not because of an indifference to what they hold to be true but because the free society as a whole, unlike its individual members, must treat cultural "truths," even the most staunchly held, as if they were tentative.

Of course the churches have their own standards of "decency" and "morality" to be upheld by their own members. The free society itself, however, necessarily has a more expansive set of standards. It also acknowledges the need for public decency and certain general criteria of morality, but in setting such standards it is obliged to heed the voices of all its members.

For instance, the fact that one or another religious group regards divorce as immoral does not mean that society is justified in banning books that uphold the possibility of divorce as a blessing. The fact that one or another group regards war as always and everywhere immoral does not mean that a movie glorifying Marines should be suppressed. Nor, by the same token, may the whole society suppress those who uphold the indissolubility of marriage or argue the merits of pacifism. As long as our society deserves to be described as free, all sides must be at liberty to propagate their views. All must be allowed to have some effect on the mass media, the publishing industry, the theatre, and the lecture platform. None, in the interests of freedom, may be encouraged to use the tactics of power to silence others.

It is the obligation of the society as a whole not only to see to it that every side is given the opportunity to state its own case but to censure those, in or out of the churches, who would prevent the expression of views inimical to their own.

We have stated that religious groups should not, especially in the name of freedom, be deprived of the freedom to apply their beliefs to the life of society. But we have also insisted that the "canons of civic prudence," to use one vocabulary, or a "respect for shared values," to use another, should govern the activities of religious groups in the world of culture.

We have emphasized that pressure-group methods, power-plays, coercion, economic boycotts, blacklisting, or threats of personal reprisals are inappropriate for religious groups operating in the cultural milieu, though they well may be strictly legal; we have pointed up the importance of persuasion in a society like ours which puts so much emphasis on individual decision and the right of all sides to receive an honest hearing.

We turn now to a question that arises out of the desire of religious groups to influence society: the relationship between the law and public morality.

Morals and the Law

The relationship between the moral imperatives preached by the churches and synagogues of Amerca and the law of the land is not easy to fix. Religious men of all faiths agree that the exercise of power must be regulated by the moral order and recognize that law itself is a moral teacher. They are united, consequently, in a conviction that there is some connection between the legal and the moral. But here unity breaks down, first, because there is no agreement on precisely what the connection between law and morals should be, secondly, because there are serious disagreements about what is and is not moral.

It is not very helpful to point out that there is a difference between a sin and a crime and stop there. For in the United States as in other Western societies, the idea of what constitutes a particular crime was often derived from the idea of a particular sin. As Norman St. John–Stevas has pointed out:[1] "The law may well preserve moral ideas long after the theology which gave rise to them has ceased to hold a general sway." He cites a number of examples, notably the law's concern with family life, which in general may be said to reflect the concept that marriage constitutes a permanent status and is not dissoluble by mere mutual consent. "Furthermore," he writes,

---

[1] In *Life, Death and the Law* (Bloomington: Indiana University Press, 1961), a volume completed under a fellowship granted by The Fund for the Republic as part of our study of religious institutions.

the law recognizes moral values not only in what it commands and punishes, but in what it refuses to countenance. Contracts made for immoral purposes are not enforceable at law. Agreements which prejudice public safety, the administration of justice, or the status of marriage are treated as being contrary to public policy and held void. Adultery, prostitution, homosexual relations, are not recognized as sources of rights by the law.

But if it is simplistic merely to distinguish between sin and crime, it is dangerous to identify the two. If all "sin" were to be punishable by law, without regard to such questions as the "sin's" effect on the common good, the enforceability of the law proscribing it, the law's effect on the right of privacy, the actual consensus existing among the people about whether or not the "sin" is sinful, and with no consideration to pertinent social facts, the result would be disastrous. Some attempts to "legislate morality" have proved the point by being spectacular failures. A classic example is America's experiment with Prohibition in the 1920's. A current example may be the laws proscribing birth control in Massachusetts and Connecticut. However well their existence originally served as a symbol of Protestant Puritan dominance in New England, and now serves as a symbol of Catholic political power in these states, these statutes are tainted with the moralism that corrupts the law. Because they are unenforceable, are held on the books against the wishes of a responsible section of the community, and do not reflect the existing consensus of the citizens who live under them, they have brought law itself into disrepute.

Even if there were general agreement on what constitutes a "sin," the arguments against turning all "sins" into "crimes" would be impressive. But of course the American people do not share a basic understanding of such matters. The Roman Catholic Church's opposition to birth control, for example, is a minority view in our society. The traditional opposition of some Protestants to all forms of gambling and drinking is not universally accepted, even in the Protestant community. Divorce, therapeutic abortion, sterilization, and euthanasia have both their supporters and their opponents among the nation's religious spokesmen as well as among the unchurched.

Differences about the sources of moral law cut even more deeply. For instance, Mr. St. John–Stevas, speaking of the Roman Catholic position propounded by modern scholars, writes:

... The State [is] a natural institution, with its own temporal end distinct from that of the Church. Individuals are bound by the natural law, and therefore the State is bound, but the State as such is not bound by the divine positive law of which it knows nothing. ... It follows that in moral as in doctrinal matters, the State is only competent to enforce the dictates of natural law.... It does not follow, however, that the State must impose every obligation of the natural law; which precepts are to be the subject of positive legislation is a political decision to be taken after full consideration of contingent social conditions.

Later, he explains that the whole concept of natural law is foreign to most Protestant thinking.

To understand Protestant ethical theory, the Catholic must first clear from his mind the whole apparatus of Aristotelian and Thomistic categories with which he has been familiar from the early days of his education and within which all his thinking has been done.

The predominant trend in Protestant ethical theory, he suggests, may have been summed up by Dr. Paul Ramsey, Chairman of the Department of Religion in Princeton University, when he wrote that Christian social ethics "becomes principally the analysis of policy and social decisions by students who have internalized the meanings of Christian revelation in faith."[2]

When there are such basic differences between important bodies of American citizens, how can the law, which binds all, reflect the religious citizen's concern for public morality? It the law is to play its traditional role of moral teacher, whose morality should it teach? If it is to be founded on pursuit of the common good, whose definition of the common good is the yardstick? If it is based on a pre-existent moral consciousness of the people, should laws be changed when the people, or a goodly section of them, have changed their minds — as minds have been changed on the questions of divorce and birth control?

The difficulties connected with the subject of morals and laws will not be dissolved in the foreseeable future. But in the meantime the arguments should continue and the basic issues be clarified so that discussion can be carried on without rancor and with a deeper understanding of what is at stake.

Our own conclusions are confined to the following:

1. Religious citizens and organized groups have a right to support the laws affecting public morality and decency that they regard

---

[2] For a view based on the insights of the Jewish tradition, see *Politics and Ethics* by Robert Gordis, (Santa Barbara, California: Center for the Study of Democratic Institutions, 1961).

as essential to the maintenance of a good society. They also have a right to work for the removal of laws they deem menacing either to freedom or to public morality.

2. All legislation, including legislation affecting public morality, should be put to sound jurisprudential tests: Is it enforceable? Will it threaten civic peace? Is it related to the common good of society and not simply to the moral perfection of individuals? Is it compatible with all the ends of our society — justice, freedom, security, a maximal margin for individual choice?

3. Religious citizens working for or against legislation should give serious consideration as to whether their proposals violate the conscientious convictions of minorities.

4. Unless a serious injury to the common good would result, majorities should not oblige minorities to follow any practice that the minority regards as immoral. This might mean, for example, that those who are conscientiously opposed to flag saluting as a form of idolatry should be left free from coercion; that those who are opposed to birth control should not be obliged to support it; that those who see evil in gambling would not be forcibly involved in a national lottery.

5. Where one group or another believes that controversial legislation of this kind might be justified by appeal to the common good, the merits and demerits of the case should be weighed in the light of the total common good, including especially the need for civic peace and friendship between citizens of differing beliefs.

6. In some cases, as in military preparedness and public health programs, the scruples of the minority will not seem to outweigh the majority's conviction that crucial decisions are at stake. But if it is at all consonant with the total good to be served, in such cases the majority would do well to make provisions in the law for conscientious objection.

We have discussed the difficulties involved in relating morality and law, noting that a nation religiously pluralistic is likely to be morally pluralistic as well. We have said that there is no wall of separation between morals and laws. At the same time, we have held that the relationship is not established by simply translating the precepts of moral teaching into legislation. The standards of jurisprudence are as applicable to legislation affecting public morality as to any other law-making.

We have stated some general rules that we believe should govern considerations of the total question. These rules are based on our conviction that not only the concern for public morality but the claims of individual consciences and desire for freedom are worthy of solemn consideration. The just claims of the society and the individual, the majority and the minority, the state and the churches, should be balanced against one another. Compromise is generally required from all parties. Though the power struggles that erupt in our kind of free society can never be, and probably never should be, totally eliminated, they can be held in check. . . .

Morality As Foreign Policy*

Kenneth W. Thompson

In the following essay Dr. Thompson, Vice-President of the Rockefeller Foundation, draws upon common strands of ethics in our political and moral heritage to derive some enduring principles upon which international peace and justice might be built. The selection was presented at a seminar program of the Council of Religion and International Affairs.

The proverbial "man from Mars" plunged suddenly onto the American continent would be treated to an amazing and confusing spectacle. He would soon discover that whereas leaders and philosophers of earlier civilizations had oftentimes stood in judgment on their people, crying out against individual and collective practices in words enshrined in a historic prophetic tradition—"thus saith the Lord"—most presentday secular and sectarian preachers reject the age-old, persistent and probably inevitable tension between ethics and foreign policy.

He would hear repeatedly that "the United States walks the path of honor alone." He would be told that for us moral force had successfully replaced power politics, selfish interests and agonizing moral dilemmas. He might even be enlisted in a moral crusade. In one word he would be informed that ethics in foreign policy is an accomplishment, not a baffling and heart-breaking problem. Yet our visitor might be excused for noting that ironically enough this national philosophy is being proclaimed in an age of unparalleled conflict, destructiveness, disorder, and strife whose imperatives touch even moral man: at Hiroshima, Budapest, Suez and on the countless battlefields of world politics yet to be.

* Reprinted from Kenneth W. Thompson, *Ethics and National Purpose* (New York: Council on Religion and International Affairs, 1957), pp. 7–18, with permission.

I believe the starting-point for a discussion of ethics and foreign policy is the quest for a secure vantage-point from which we can perceive that many of our moral judgments are at best premature. Man at root is not only, as for Aristotle, a social and political animal. He is also a moral being. He cannot eschew moral judgments. Yet since his virtue and knowledge are limited, his moral valuations are fragmentary and partial. Moreover, contemporary social scientists like Max Weber have pointed to a hidden and neglected truth regarding moral claims. Since moral men seek moral reasons and justifications for their acts, they are endlessly tempted to invest aspirations, interests and conduct with ethical meaning.

For Weber, men cover their purely selfish pursuits with a tissue of lies and deception meant to convey their virtue. Ideologies are fabricated to justify political conduct to others. It must be said that the notion that an ideal is never more than rationalization is carried too far when men deny the differences between good and bad political ideas or equate the potentially healthy myths of democracy and the demoniac ones of totalitarianism. Yet it is also true that history is strewn with moral claims convincing at the time but seen now as at best a shrewd mixture of good and evil, of aspiration and aggrandizement, of uplift and grosser human qualities. Man's powers of self-deception are seemingly endless.

The Moral Dilemma

At the heart of this problem is a moral dilemma. We are never as moral as we claim to be. This is true of the parent who disciplines the child "for its own good" no less than of the powerful nation who works its will on less powerful, but no less virtuous, states. Even when justice is the goal of a loving father it invariably becomes mixed with coercion, caprice and injustice. The Athenian envoys to Melos, who were perhaps more transparently honest than some of their latter-day successors, said of a powerful rival: "Of all the men we know they are most conspicuous in considering what is agreeable—honorable and what is expedient—just." Centuries later the historian Dicey found that in Western society "men come easily to believe that arrangements agreeable to themselves are beneficial to others."

Nations with few exceptions have seen their cause and supremacy as equivalent to universal justice. Lord Wolseley maintained

I have but one great object in this world, and that is to maintain the greatness of the Empire. But apart from my John Bull sentiment upon the point, I firmly believe that in doing so I work in the cause of Christianity, of peace, of civilization, and the happiness of the human race generally.

Or in 1935 in an early phase of his writings, Professor Arnold J. Toynbee discovered that the security of the British Empire "was also the supreme interest of the whole world." The Archbishop of Canterbury at the time of the Italian aggression in Ethiopia admonished the French: "We are animated by moral and spiritual considerations ... It is ... no egoist interest driving us forward, and no consideration of interest should keep you behind." However, more sober historians looking today for the cause of the paralysis of French policy and its failure to act point not to her moral depravity but to a tragic and tangled procession of events that includes our refusal to give guarantees, a pathological fear of Germany, and a plausible but ill-fated attempt to gain security in the Northeast through an *entente* with Italy in the South. As partners in two world wars with the British we perhaps find their claims more plausible than the assertion of a prominent National Socialist in 1935: "Anything that benefits the German people is right, anything that harms the German people is wrong."

Nor is American history lacking in comparable examples. It provides the story of President McKinley, who spent the night in prayer for divine guidance before deciding, as one might have expected, to annex the Philippines. Or President Wilson, who, following the bombardment of Vera Cruz in 1914, assured the world that "the United States had gone to Mexico to serve mankind," and who shortly before our entry into World War I identified American principles and American policies as "the principles of mankind ... [which] must prevail." We are reminded of De Toqueville's words:

> If I say to an American that the country he lives in is a fine one, aye, he replies and there is not its equal in the world. If I applaud the freedom its inhabitants enjoy, he answers "freedom is a fine thing but few nations are worthy of it." If I remark on the purity of morals that distinguishes the United States he declares "I can imagine that a stranger who has witnessed the corruption which prevails in other nations would be astonished at the difference." At length I leave him to a contemplation of himself, but he returns to the charge and does not desist until he has got me to repeat all I have been saying. It is impossible to conceive a more troublesome and garrulous patriotism.

Spiritual Pride

It should, of course, be obvious that every nation has its own form of spiritual pride, its own peculiar version. Our version is compounded, I would suppose, of at least three factors.

The first derives from the role of the immigrant who had turned his back on the vices of Europe and was making a new beginning. Having shaken the dust of the Old World from his feet, he was anxious to prove that none of its ancient failings were his failings. Their purposes, often sullied by the ambiguities and compromises bound up with national existence in the cockpit of Europe, were not his purposes. And strikingly enough, his affirmations of moral purity —or more specifically, those by which national leaders appealed to his virtue—seemed to be confirmed by early American social history. In the first phases of this history the frontier saved us from the acrimony of class struggle and, later, our superior technology gave new outlets to the ambitious and adventurous. Beyond this we were freed from international responsibility and a European equilibrium of power which British policy and naval power were dedicated to preserve. In such a world, it was natural to assume that domestic policies were more important than foreign policy and that the alliances so prevalent on the European scene were an expensive and pernicious nuisance. These objective conditions have passed but the psychology they inspired lingers on, as in the recent sweeping and indignant denunciations of the exercise of power by European states followed abruptly by our own decision to use force unilaterally if necessary in the Middle East.

Legalism

A second factor shaping the American outlook results from the fact that our prevailing philosophy of international relations has been a curious blending of legalism and rationalism. Law and reason are of course indispensable ingredients of an orderly life. They are precious fruits of the flowering of a free community and the good life. And ultimately peace becomes inevitable only when law and order prevail. However, the tragedy of much of our thinking has been to assume this ultimate end was either realized or shortly realizable and to tailor our words and sometimes our deeds to fit this mistaken assumption.

American lawyers whose influence on our foreign relations has been immense have confused the realities of municipal law with the hopes of international law. They have imposed on the international system burdens it could not bear. If the problem was war, it must be outlawed (the Kellogg–Briand Pact). If the peril was aggression, a legal formula proscribing and defining it was the goal—even though a United Nations Commission recently gave up this task in despair. If states trembled in a state of insecurity, reassure them with security pacts heaped one upon the other! If a state threatened the peace, pass a resolution! All these acts, so frequently a positive force in organized and integrated communities, have on balance weakened the feeble system of international order, for pacts, declarations and formulas at odds with the realities of international life tempt the lawless to reckless adventures and the law-abiding to a whole chain of emotional responses beginning with self-righteousness and indignation, shading off into disillusionment and finally into despair.

Legalists brush aside the limits of international law and the fact that it is still in a laissez-faire stage of development. J. L. Brierly, one of the half-dozen lawyers in the twentieth century whose writings have an enduring quality, begins his little classic *The Outlook for International Law* with the following quotation from John Morley:

> Success in politics, as in every other art, obviously before all else implies both knowledge of the material with which we have to deal, and also such concession as is necessary to the qualities of the materials. Above all, in politics we have an art in which development depends upon small modifications. . . . To hurry on after logical perfection is to show oneself ignorant of the material. . . . To disdain anything short of an organic change in thought or institution is infatuation.

Then he concludes:

> . . . The part that international law can play, or the conditions on which we can hope to make it one of the pillars of a more stable world, cannot be determined by reasoning in the void or by wishful thinking. Too many people assume, generally without having given any serious thought to its character or history, that international law is and always has been a sham. Others seem to think that it is a force with inherent strength of its own, and that if we only had the sense to set the lawyers to work to draft a comprehensive code for the nations, we might live together in peace and all would be well with the world. Whether the cynic or the sciolist is the less helpful is hard to say . . .

Unhappily for us, historians will search in vain for this modesty and maturity in the legalist approach to American foreign policy. At times the very virtues of the legal approach in a society with effective

legislatures and courts have become the vices of international life,
e.g. case-by-case diplomacy.

Rationalism

If we have suffered from legalism, the price of liberal rationalism
has been still greater. It has been said of the League of the United
Nations that they represent an attempt to apply the principles of
Lockean liberalism to the machinery of international order. They
carry into world affairs the outlook of a liberal democratic society.
One rather acute critic has noted in some rational spokesmen the
tendency to believe that there can exist a card index of situations
or events to be consulted for the appropriate and prescribed action
whenever the event or situation turns up. Standardized procedures
are valued more than prudence, the perfection of machinery more
than political wisdom. Four decades of experience in transplanting
liberal rationalism to the world scene have taught that this approach
can be full of unforeseen difficulties.

This is not the place to discuss these problems except to suggest
that where prestige of states is involved, rational discussion need
not necessarily be served by open forums. Mr. Lester Pearson has
written with great insight and judgment of the problems of diplomacy in a "goldfish bowl." Moreover, responsible international conduct is not the necessary result of gathering together representatives
of some eighty states differing widely in size, in power, and in
political, economic and cultural developments. States not affected
by events and not required to sacrifice vital interests can more easily
strike poses than those whose security is in jeopardy. Nations with
limited interests in a question may band together to outvote states
whose survival may be at stake. For example, it would be helpful to
know how often uninstructed UN delegates on matters of no concern
to their government throw their votes capriciously to the support
of a resolution for which they would be unwilling to accept direct
national responsibility. It would be useful to discover how often
states turn to the United Nations when they are unwilling or unable
to evolve a viable foreign policy of their own.

To ask such questions is not to detract from the vital and construc-
tive role of the United Nations. However, if this new international
institution is to survive and grow, its members must face the hard
problems. They must recognize that it provides a set of methods and
procedures and embodies certain fundamental aims and goals. However, it can contribute only what its members bring to its affairs in
the form of policies, resources and loyalties. It will not, in the fore-

seeable future, be a substitute for foreign policy, and we should remind ourselves continually of this when we are tempted to drop the hard issues and unsolved problems in its lap.

One observer has argued: "When the government of the United States is asked, What is your policy for the Middle East? and it replies, We shall act through the United Nations, it has only replied to the procedural question and still owes an answer to the all-important question, What is your United Nations policy for the Middle East?" Former Secretary of State Dean Acheson, in a statement to the House Foreign Affairs Committee, declared last year:

> It will not do to say that the United Nations will determine policy, make decisions, and enforce them. The United Nations is not a supranational entity with a mind, a will and a power. It is a forum, and no more than the nations which meet there. Nothing more comes out of it than is put into it. If a great nation, like the United States, looks to the United Nations to form American policy, instead of fighting in the United Nations for what the American Government believes should be done, then we have committed an unprecedented abdication of responsibility and power. We deserve what we get. If we believe that we have exhausted our responsibilities when we join in the United Nations to pass resolutions which are defied, and which we have no intention of backing up, we have engaged in a most dangerous form of self-deception.

For modern man, this view of the United Nations or similar conceptions of other cherished institutions are anathema. Rationalism's twin gods are progress and human perfectibility. For Diderot "posterity is for the philosopher what the other world is for the religious." For Comte the advance of human knowledge would eliminate human conflict by "inculcating in all men the same principles of virtue and goodness." For Condorcet progress was such a certainty that he could write his *Outline of the Progress of the Human Spirit* at a time he himself was a fugitive from the guillotine of the French Revolution.

According to the liberal or rationalist world view, evil in history is ascribable to social institutions or ignorance or some other manageable defect in the human environment. It is *not* the product of human nature. Correct the institution and man's problems are solved. The United Nations was designed to rectify the evils of traditional world politics. It was packaged and sold on this basis. Therefore when we have redress to the methods and measures by which states continue to make their way, the rationalist is offended.

Indeed, nothing has been more disabling in America's adjustment to her new world responsibilities than the over-dependence on this liberal rationalist point of view.

Sectarianism

A third source of American pride is the regnant theme of our sectarian religious outlook. Whether for New England Calvinism and the Deism of Jefferson in Virginia, or more recently for much of modernist Protestant and Catholic thought, this land has been identified as God's "American Israel." With all its pessimism about human nature, Calvinism, in the words of Edward Johnson in *Wonder Working Province of Zion's Saviour* (1650), found here "the place where the Lord would create a new heaven and a new earth, new churches and a new commonwealth." Here the Protestant Reformation had reached its final culmination and here God had made a new beginning for mankind. The Deist's God was nature's God, and Jefferson, whose thought was a blending of religious faith and Enlightenment rationalism, could assert: "Before the establishment of the American States nothing was known to history but the man of the old world crowded within limits . . . and steeped in vices which the situation generates." Superior virtue was an outgrowth of favorable social circumstances and the distinction between Europe and America was an absolute one.

It is the religious dimension of America's pride that brings us to the crux of the problem of ethics and foreign policy. Historically, religion when it has not been used as an instrument of self-righteousness has provided the one firm base from which to view man's moral dilemma. This is true on the one hand because religion almost alone gives the resources for reconciling the majesty and misery of life. It accepts sin and salvation as a datum of life, and at least in its profoundest insights is not forever consumed in proving that through this artifact or that we can escape from the moral dilemma.

This dilemma in foreign policy is but a special, though a particularly flagrant, example of the moral dilemma facing men on all levels of social action. Man cannot help sinning when he acts in relation to his fellow men; he may be able to minimize that sinfulness but he cannot escape it. For no social action can be completely free of the taint of egotism which, as selfishness, pride, or self-deception, claims for the actor more than is his due. Man's aspiration for power over other men, which is of the essence of politics, tends toward the denial of the very core of Judeo-Christian morality. That is the historic precept of respect for man as an end in himself.

The power relation in any ultimate sense is a denial of this respect, for power at root involves the use of man as a means to the end of another man. The full pathos of this appears on the international scene where the civilizing influences of law, morality and mores are less effective than on the domestic political scene. And paradoxically, while nations take this for granted and appraise the power drives of others for what they are or worse, they blind themselves to their own aspirations, which appear as something different and nobler—justified by necessity and ethics. The Founding Fathers were more sensitive to this than some moderns, for it was John Adams who wrote:

> Power always thinks it has a great soul and vast views beyond the comprehension of the weak and that it is doing God's service when it is violating all His laws. Our passions, ambitions, avarice, love and resentment, etc., possess so much metaphysical subtlety and so much overpowering eloquence that they insinuate themselves into the understanding and the conscience and convert both to their party.

Religion has not only contributed the intellectual and spiritual resources for understanding the moral dilemma. It has also at times in Western history check-mated the extravagances of temporal authority. The struggles between emperors and popes are only the most dramatic expression of the use of a countervailing moral and political power. Probably this resistance has been most successful when the claims of princes and rulers were made in the name of higher moral principles which could be judged by certain accepted moral and legal standards based on an objective external authority. With the passing of the *corpus Christianum* this explicit authority, at least for parts of the world, seems to have disappeared. The substitutes thus far discovered are but pale reflections, for they no longer rest on a substantial moral consensus. It is symptomatic of the times that Ambassador Dillon perhaps indiscreetly reported that the French withdrawal from Suez was due not to the pressure of moral force but to the Russian ultimatum. It may also have resulted from economic coercion and political pressure in the West.

If nations are obliged to consider their own interests, they also must attend to the interests of others. This note is struck in Number 63 of the Federalist papers:

An attention to the judgment of other nations is important to every government for two reasons: the one is, that, independently of the merits of any particular plan or measure, it is desirable on various accounts, that it should appear to other nations as the off-spring of a wise and honourable policy; the second is, that in doubt-ful cases, particularly where the national councils may be warped by some strong passion or momentary interest, the presumed or known opinion of the impartial world may be the best guide that can be followed. What has not America lost by her want of character with foreign nations; and how many errors and follies would she not have avoided if the justice and propriety of her measures had, in every instance, been previously tried by the light in which they would probably appear to the unbiased part of mankind.

The same may be said of other nations as well. Nevertheless, plainly we are groping for new forms of ethical restraint on inter-national conduct and for the rediscovery of old forms of international morality. In conclusion, I may perhaps suggest half a dozen areas in which this may be the case.

Ideas and Realities

First, it seems to have dawned upon even the more cynical among us that there are certain points at which expediency and morality meet. Put in negative and pragmatic terms, we recall the words of the Athenian envoys to Melos: "And it is certain that those who do not yield to their equals, who keep terms with their superiors, and are moderate towards their inferiors, on the whole best suc-ceed." Seen more positively, the Marshall Plan and other postwar efforts are attempts to find points of coincidence between our inter-ests and those of our allies.

Second, we note in the conduct of our relations with representa-tives of other states that confidence, patience, dignity and restraint comprise the cement without which the sturdiest alliance will crumble. It is too much to expect that nations will show gratitude or lasting affection for one another. Generosity is as likely to produce envy, resentment and contempt as to create goodwill, for no govern-ment based on popular support can afford to acknowledge the full scale of its independence on others. Yet there are bonds which can flourish and develop between states which show a decent respect for the dignity and interests of one another. Nor are the personal factors inconsequential. Diplomats may be honest men sent abroad "to lie in the interest of their country," yet they must return to negotiate another day.

One of the factors contributing to peace in an earlier day was the union among members of an aristocratic elite who belonged to the same club, spoke the same language, shared the same values (such as they were) and enjoyed a rough and ready assurance that everyone would keep his word. Even if it were imaginable, no one would wish today to reconstruct the past, yet this aspect of nineteenth century experience contains a profound lesson. Peace is the outcome of mutual confidence and respect. The moral basis for such confidence may be lacking today, say, with the Communist envoys, yet the breakdown of confidence among Western leaders who found they could not trust one another is a more tragic example of the price that must be paid for failure here.

Third, the pathway toward implementing and effecting the values we cherish is a tangled and tortuous road on which we can almost never see the end nor the immediate terrain we traverse. Yet, with halting steps some of our friends have quietly found their way. Austria, following the peace treaty, accepted a neutralist role that was offensive to some in the West who preferred that nations stand up and be counted. It would be hard to prove that her contribution to freedom in recent history could have been any greater had she chosen our directive. Yugoslavia has caused us special anguish, but at the same time set an example for the Satellites that in the long run may be decisive for the West. In much the same way, we face some painful choices in the times ahead. Should we insist that Arab countries accept a new security system as the price of technical assistance? Should we demand that Western Germany retain her membership in NATO even at the expense of reunification? What about our policy toward the Satellites? What is the road to freedom?

Fourth, there are the first faint signs of an emerging set of common values at the United Nations. It is tempting to associate them with those embodied in the Declaration of Independence. The discovery is reassuring that the leader of a great Asian state could share a common universe of discourse with an American President even though they may also share common illusions. The values which have meaning in the practice of the United Nations remain in any detail a mystery. Yet they perhaps involve some appreciation of the principles of justice, of consent of the governed, of peace and of social progress. We can only guess as to the context of these values in practice until we know more than we now do.

Fifth, we have ample proof, if that were needed, that in foreign affairs there is not one ethical principle, but many. Peace is a value but so are security and honor. Freedom from colonialism is a goal but so are order and safeguards against tyranny. Support for the rising colored peoples and the underprivileged of the world is a noble purpose but so is the defense of Western civilization. There is no moral touchstone that can help us judge in advance which goal should be served. Nor can we subordinate all aims to one master goal—for all time. There can be no choice but to view them from the ground on which we stand, members of a nation that we are pledged to serve and defend but whose pretenses and failings must also be judged. The ancients in such a situation called for practical wisdom, and we recall Lincoln's words that he knew no other guide than to do the best he could and would go on doing so until the end.

Sixth, the most hopeful step toward understanding is an awareness that political morality, not morality *in abstract* is what we seek. We have begun to resurrect from the rubble of false philosophies which did not stand the test of time the great perennial truths about politics and morality of which Western civilization is the record. We have learned in the aftermath of two world wars and through the agony of waging the Cold War for peace that we cannot escape the temptations and liabilities of power politics by a simple act of will. We now perceive that we must live in a brutal world and still remain civilized. We must live in an immoral world and make the best of it. Yet even at best we cannot forget that these burdens and temptations are ever with us.

Perhaps the full poignancy of the tension between ethics and foreign policy is seen in the sphere of Soviet–American relations. What do we propose to do about the signs of breakup in the Communist world? Is this a problem where ethics play no role? I think one can look at this problem through the screen of a simple and abstract point of view, a cynical point of view and one which perhaps combines wisdom and morality. The consequences for history are grave and far-reaching. A simple and abstract point of view would prompt us to pursue a policy of active, outspoken liberation. It would revive the boisterous claims and righteous affirmations of the 1952 election campaign. A cynical view would abandon East Europeans to their fate.

Practical Wisdom

Fortunately, we may have a third, less futile or dismal alternative. It has been described by one of our wisest diplomatists as that of liberation through negotiations and disengagement, rather than bloody civil or global conflict. The estimate of Soviet foreign policy on which it is based is, of course, open to debate, for the Russians may be resolved to follow a policy of oppression whenever resistance raises its head. On the other hand, they may conceive it to be in their interest to withdraw from Eastern Europe when they can do so without too much loss of face. A situation that could make this feasible might arise tomorrow, next year or a decade from now. At some time, however, they might consider that Communist prestige could be preserved if, as part of a political settlement, they yield up their claims to base troops in the Satellites for some form of military or political concession from the West, perhaps as part of the creation of a Europe-wide security program. This might conceivably involve the withdrawal of Western forces from Germany and the establishment of a neutralized zone in Central Europe.

Perhaps the prospect of a political settlement is illusory and surely any plan for neutralization would raise serious problems for the West. Yet, the states of Eastern Europe freed from the grinding control of the ever-present Red Army might over time evolve as have other neutral states in the direction of freedom. If so, a policy of restraint would bring victory to freedom over tyranny without the grave risks that other courses of action entail. Thus a prudent policy based on the dictates of practical wisdom might be in the end the most moral course we could follow.